SO-BSH-396

What Readers are saying about
A Treasury of Truth and Wisdom

"In a day when multitudes of platitudes fill the air, here is a treasure chest of resplendent jewels, displayed in the uncomplicated simplicity of life-giving truth and ageless wisdom."

James Ryle, Founder
Truth Works Ministry

"Fred Slicker is a layman who believes in the power and simplicity of God's Word. His crisp and concise writing style is refreshing. If you are stuck and need to be revitalized, *Treasury* will be a real encouragement to your spiritual life."

Dr. Ken Canfield, Founder
National Center for Fathering

"*A Treasury of Truth and Wisdom* collects time-tested truths and puts them in modern but profoundly simple statements of wisdom. *Treasury* should be on every businessman's daily reading list."

Robert Parker, Sr., Chairman
Parker Drilling Company

"*Treasury* reads like a modern day book of Proverbs. They are true principles of life, validated by the experience of a seasoned businessman."

Peter Enns, President
Good Word Publications
"America's Poet"

Additional copies of this book are available

online at amazon.com,

at your local bookstore,

or at www.fredslicker.com

A Treasury
of
Truth and Wisdom

A Treasury of Truth and Wisdom. Copyright © 2007, 2008 by Frederick K. Slicker, 4444 East 66th Street, Suite 201, Tulsa, OK 74136-4206. All rights reserved.

All Scripture quotations are taken from the *Holy Bible, New International Translation* ® NIV ®. Copyright © 1973, 1978, 1984 by International Bible Society. Used by permission. All rights reserved.

The "NIV" and "New International Version" trademarks are registered in the United States Patent and Trademark Office by the International Bible Society. Use of either trademark requires the permission of the International Bible Society, and commercial use of either term requires the permission of Zondervan Publishing.

ISBN 978-0-88144-269-4
Published by Thorncrown Publishing
A Division of Yorkshire Publishing Group
7707 East 111th, Suite 104
Tulsa, OK 74133
www.yorkshirepublishing.com

Cover design by D. Tucker

Page design by Diane Whisner

Printed in Canada. All rights are reserved under International Copyright Law. Neither the contents nor the cover may be reproduced in whole or in part in any form without the express prior written consent of Frederick K. Slicker. Requests for such consent may be made to Frederick K. Slicker, 4444 East 66th Street, Suite 201, Tulsa, OK 74136-4206, telephone 918-496-9020, fax 918-496-9024, e-mail: fred@slickerlawfirm.com.

Subject Index

Dedication

To Laura, Luke, Eli, Kipp and Chris.
May your lives be filled with
the Joy and Peace
of Truth and Wisdom.

**"I have no greater joy than to hear that
my children are walking in the truth."**
3 John 4

Introduction

Truth is a treasure to be embraced. Truth is factual, objective and provable. Truth is not an idea some where between two opposing opinions. There is not a Republican truth and a Democratic truth. Truth is truth, no matter who says it. Wisdom is truth tested by time and subjected to moral judgment. Wisdom answers questions, such as: What is good? What is desirable? and What is sacred?

Our contemporary culture has confused us by embracing the popular notions of moral relativism, rugged individualism and situational ethics. Too often today, what is true varies with the circumstances; what is right is blurred by culture, politics and religion; and what is wise depends upon a point of view, rather than a moral imperative.

A *Treasury of Truth and Wisdom* challenges the contemporary notions that truth depends on the circumstances and that wisdom is fluid floating on a sea of relativism.

Treasury is a collection of fundamental truths and nuggets of wisdom which teach, guide, encourage and lead the reader in times of uncertainty and difficulty. *Treasury* consists of a treasure chest overflowing with time-tested truth and insights for living a life of wisdom. When embraced, the ideas found in *Treasury* will inevitably lead to a life of significance, joy and peace.

Everyone faces obstacles, and everyone experiences adversity. To the high school student, there are college entrance exams to conquer. To the college student, there is tuition to pay, scholarships to receive, loans to obtain and final exams to pass. For the graduate, the right job must be pursued and secured. The overly demanding boss and the long hours separate the young professional from his family. For the boss, there are customer demands to meet, competitors to beat, invoices to collect and bills to pay. To the widow, health issues abound. To the elderly, aging and death are constant companions. Everyone faces challenges. Obstacles and adversity are a natural part of the journey of life.

". . . call upon me in the day of trouble; I will deliver you. . . ."

Psalm 50:15

Thank God! Without competitors to confront, we would not know the joy of winning. Without the obstacles, we would believe that we do not need God or others. Without adversity, we could not comprehend the healing power of God. Without the challenges, life would not be worth the effort of living. Thank God for the challenges we face, for the difficulties we must endure and for the adversity we must overcome, for it is in persevering, enduring and overcoming that we experience true joy.

Obstacles can break the weak.
Adversity makes the wise strong.

How we handle adversity reflects
the depth of our character.

Unless we try, we will never conquer
our fear of uncertainty and failure.
When we try, we will learn to
overcome our fear, even if we fail.

A predicate for growth is overcoming hardship.
The greater the opposition,
the greater the reward in overcoming it.

The fool sees a rainy day.
The wise use the rain to cleanse their souls.

The young experience suffering and ask,
"Why is this happening to me?"
The mature overcome suffering and say,
"Without the suffering, I could not have
received this blessing."

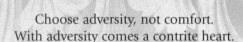

Choose adversity, not comfort.
With adversity comes a contrite heart.

Overcome adversity with
excitement and determination.
Overcome obstacles with perseverance and persistence.

The proud see their own importance
in overcoming obstacles.
The wise see the footprint of God in the victories won.

When tested, the timid lose control
over their emotions.
The wise demonstrate poise in the face of adversity.

A gem is polished by rubbing it.
Man grows by overcoming adversity.

Metal is purified by fire.
Man is purified by testing.

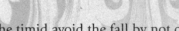

The timid avoid the fall by not climbing at all.
The wise get up after the fall to climb again.

Failure is a temporary condition of life.
A life without failure is a life without achievement.

The greatest obstacle for man to conquer
is to know himself.
The hardest test for any man is to overcome himself.

The fool complains about obstacles and adversity.
The wise view obstacles as opportunities to overcome.

Man comes closest to God through pain and suffering.
Spiritual growth follows trials, tests and failures.

The wicked overcome adversity on the backs of others.
The wise conquer difficulties for the benefit of others.

The weak quit when the going gets tough.
The wise persevere in tough times.

The greatest thoughts,
the greatest discoveries,
the greatest inventions and
the greatest creations of man
have all arisen out of adversity.

Every human achievement involves
overcoming firmly held beliefs
and time honored ways.
Achievement cannot occur
without change, criticism and uncertainty.

If life were without trials,
how would our faith in God grow?
If life were without adversity,
how would we ever know God's power?
If life were without pain,
how would we ever know God's healing?
If life were without obstacles,
how would we ever know God's peace?
If life were perfect,
why would we need God?

Adversity and Obstacles

". . . we also rejoice in our sufferings, because we know
that suffering produces perseverance; perseverance,
character; and character, hope. And hope does not
disappoint us. . . ."
Romans 5:3-5

"Who shall separate us from the love of Christ?
Shall trouble or hardship or persecution or
famine or nakedness or danger or sword? . . .
No, in all these things we are more than
conquerors through him who loved us.
For I am convinced that neither death
nor life, neither angels nor demons,
neither the present nor the future,
nor any powers, neither height nor depth,
nor anything else in all creation,
will be able to separate us from the love of God
that is in Christ Jesus our Lord."
Romans 8:35,37-39

"This is love for God: to obey his commandments.
And his commandments are not burdensome,
for everyone born of God overcomes the world."
1 John 5:3-4

"He who has an ear, let him hear what the Spirit
says to the churches. To him who overcomes,
I will give the right to eat from the tree of life,
which is in the paradise of God."
Revelation 2:7

We are generally quick to give advice to others, to suggest solutions, to list alternatives, to fix the problem. We are especially vulnerable to the "fix it" mentality. After all, we are trained to confront the competitor, to engage in battle and to win the victory. We tend to be problem solvers, counselors, advisors. Giving advice demonstrates our vast experience, our superior knowledge and our unique understanding and importance. But we are generally not good listeners. We speak when we should just listen.

> *"Let the wise listen and add to their learning,*
> *and let the discerning get guidance. . ."*
>
> Proverbs 1:5

All of us need to take the time and make the effort to really listen to others. Listening is the first step in understanding their difficulties, in feeling their pain and in healing their hurts. Compassion and caring are hollow without listening, really listening to others.

Being still is also the only way we can slow down and listen to our own spirit. Finding that still place, sometimes called the thin place, and being quiet enable us to commune with our souls and hear the voice of God.

The words of the wicked lead to destruction.
The actions of the wise bring comfort and peace.

The words of the wicked cut to the quick.
The words of the righteous build up hope.

A blowhard inherits his own wind.
A blowhard reaps what he blows.

Consider the counsel of the wise.
Reject the advice of the fool.

The shallow speak continually.
The wise listen carefully.

Be quick to listen, slow to judge.
Be quick to care, slow to compare.

The fool freely shouts his opinions.
The wise opine only when asked.

The fool speaks up.
The wise listen up.

The art of listening requires that you hear
what is being said and what is not being said.

Listen to the voice within you.
Your conscience is an excellent guide.

The speed of daily life makes listening difficult.
Slow down and listen to life carefully.

You have to be near to hear cries for help.
It is critical to listen carefully to hear with compassion.

Too much advice can result in deadlock.
Listen to the wisdom of the mature and reject the
outcry of the young.

Consider the source of the advice you receive.
Follow the words of the wise.
Reject the counsel of the fool.

Advice is rarely welcomed, even when sought.
Those who seek advice welcome it least.

Advice would be more accepted
if it followed what we want anyway.

He who seeks advice seeks a
collaborator and an accomplice.

The fool gives men his voice.
The wise give others his ear.

The fool needs advice but rarely takes it.
The wise consider advice but rarely need it.

The fool is a great talker and a little doer.
The wise are great doers and little talkers.

The fool is quick to speak, quick to judge and
quick to compare. The wise are quick to affirm,
quick to listen and quick to praise.

Gossip and rumors capture the interest of the fool.
The wise repeat only the truth.

The proud hear the praises of men.
The wise listen for the affirmation of God.

Advice and Listening

"The way of a fool seems right to him,
but a wise man listens to advice."
Proverbs 12:15

"He who answers before listening—
that is his folly and his shame."
Proverbs 18:13

"Everyone should be quick to listen,
slow to speak and slow to become angry . . .
Do not merely listen to the word,
and so deceive yourselves. Do what it says."
James 1:19,22

Attitude is the stance you take, the position you articulate, the tone of your voice, the focus of your eyes, the presence you bring to the table. Every action you take and every omission you avoid contains an expression of your attitude. And your attitude dramatically affects the attitude of others you meet. If you are angry, their joy will be hidden from you. If you are jealous, your desires will be apparent in their rejection of you. If you are filled with sorrow, others will be sad in your presence. If you seek to blame, others will find fault in you. If you are filled with lies, others will hide the truth from you. The response you receive is a reflection of your attitude. You get back what you give out.

> *"You turned my wailing into dancing; you removed my sackcloth and clothed me with joy."*
>
> Psalm 30:11

If you want to experience joy, give off a sense of joy. If you want to find peace, let your attitude reflect the peace of your countenance. If you desire hope, promote positive possibilities with exuberance. If you hope to enjoy faith, demonstrate reverence. If you seek love, you must show love for others. None of us can control what happens to us. However, each of us has total control over the attitude we display in the face of what happens to us. Let your attitude so shine that all those around you are filled with joy, hope, peace and love.

Attitude is a choice.
Choose wisely and keep it positive.

Some say "Why?"
Others say "Why not!"

Some say "If only. . . ."
Others say "Next time. . . ."

Some smell the barn and dread the cleanup.
Others anticipate the ride of the horse to be saddled.

Arrogance and guilt are common
companions of the fool.
The wise are rich in humility and long in forgiveness.

Keep your song in the air.
No one likes to be around a grump!

It is not possible to control what happens to you.
It is possible to control your attitude
about what happens.

Criticism corrupts.
Praise builds up.

An attitude of humility and thankfulness
yields a grateful heart.

Everyone prefers a cheerful attitude, not a bitter pill.
An ill temper serves no one's tastes or desires.

The fool wants what he cannot have
and belittles what he already has.
The wise are content with what they cannot have
and grateful for what they do have.

The fool accepts passivity and sheds responsibility.
The wise reject passivity and accept responsibility.

A cheerful spirit brings a glow to others.
A critical attitude smothers the joy in others.

The fool complains and criticizes.
The wise affirm and praise.

An attitude of adventure makes every journey fun.
An attitude of "have to" pollutes the "want to" within.

An attitude of respect for others
will make them friends.
An attitude of superiority will turn
others into adversaries.

Criticism is negative. Avoid it like the plague.
Praise is positive. Share it like the rarest of gifts.

Attitude

"A cheerful look brings joy to the heart. . . ."
Proverbs 15:30

"A cheerful heart is good medicine, but
a crushed spirit dries up bones."
Proverbs 17:22

"Gladness and joy will overtake them,
and sorrow and sighing will flee away."
Isaiah 51:11

"Do everything without complaining or arguing,
so that you may become blameless and pure. . . ."
Philippians 2:14-15

"I can do everything through him
who gives me strength."
Philippians 4:13

We have the awesome power and free will to choose. That is the good part. The potentially bad part is that there are always consequences to the choices we make. We must bear those consequences, whether our choices prove to be sound or whether those choices prove to be misguided. With the freedom to choose comes the responsibility to live with the consequences that result from those choices.

Some choices are easy, and some are difficult. Some choices result in riches, and some prove financially disastrous. Some choices result in love, joy, peace and happiness, while others lead to a life of addiction, injury and agony. Some choices have consequences that only affect you, but other choices affect you, your family, friends and others. The freedom to choose is an awesome gift. Choose wisely, and you will be blessed and be a blessing to others. Choose poorly, and you can cause untold anguish, anger, disappointment and injury. It is your choice.

> *"This day I call heaven and earth as witnesses against you that I have set before you life and death, blessings and curses. Now choose life, so that you and your children may live and that you may love the Lord your God, listen to his voice, and hold fast to him."*
>
> Deuteronomy 30:19-20

We get to choose what we say, what we do
and who we become. Choose wisely.

God's greatest gift to man is free will.
Free will includes the power to choose badly.
Choose wisely.

Do not wait for opportunities to come your way.
Seize the opportunities now before you.

This very moment is pregnant with possibilities.
You can change your life by changing your choices.

You must be willing to give up what you have
to get what you want. Not choosing is a choice.

Freedom lies not in the quantity of your possessions
but in the quality of your choices.

Choose to be the spark of excitement,
not the wet blanket of criticism or doubt.

Choose to be the candle that lights the darkness,
not the curse that condemns the vision.

You have the awesome power to choose:
To fight or surrender;
To move forward or backward;
To smile or frown;
To accept or reject;
To love or hate;
To hurt or heal;
To give or withhold;
To forgive or hold a grudge;
To tell the truth or lie;
To cheat or follow the rules;
To win or lose;
To live or die.
The choice is yours.
Choose wisely.

Choose impossible dreams to pursue,
not goals that are too small, too easy, too low.

Choose to:
Be honest in all things;
Be flexible to withstand the storms of change;
Be happy in work or choose to do something else;
Be curious, so that you are constantly learning;
Be focused on what is important now;
Be faithful to God, to others and then to yourself;
Be a peacemaker and a problem-solver;
Be positive in all things;
Be a friend to those in need;
Be grateful and generous;
Be yourself, not what others want you to be;
Be the best you can be.

The quality of your life is defined by
the quality of the choices you make.

Life is a journey.
There will be storms.
There will be sunshine.
There will be failures.
There will be victories.
The quality of your life is defined by
how you react to the changes you experience.

You can chose to be right or wrong.
You can choose to speak or remain silent.
You can choose to work or sleep.
You can choose to eat or starve.
You can choose to help or hurt.
You can choose to create or copy.
You can choose to learn or be ignorant.
You can choose to have faith or doubt.
You can choose to build up or tear down.
You can choose to criticize or to encourage.
You can choose to give or withhold.
You can choose to love or hate.
Your choices will define your life.
The choice is yours.

Choices

"But if serving the Lord seems undesirable to you,
then choose for yourselves this day whom
you will serve . . . But as for me and
my household, we will serve the Lord."
Joshua 24:15

"Choose my instruction instead of silver,
knowledge rather than choice gold, for
wisdom is more precious than rubies,
and nothing you desire can compare with her."
Proverbs 8:10-11

We are quick to criticize and slow to praise. We often distinguish ourselves from others by comparing, contrasting and criticizing others. We are often slow to accentuate the positive traits of others in an effort to elevate what we want others to think about us. Judging others without looking soberly at ourselves is self-deluding and self-defeating.

"You, therefore, have no excuse, you who pass judgment on someone else, for at whatever point you judge the other, you are condemning yourself, because you who pass judgment do the same things."

Romans 2:1

It is much easier to criticize than to build up. It is much simpler to find fault in others than to correct bigger faults in ourselves. Pride, arrogance and selfishness are at the heart of how we see ourselves and how we look at others. When we free ourselves of being negative about others, we miraculously find we are more positive, more pleasant and more hopeful about ourselves. When we stop criticizing and comparing ourselves with others, we free ourselves of the gossip and the critiques we share with others.

Reject comparisons of others to elevate yourself.
Reflect soberly upon yourself before criticizing others.

Compare not, that you are not found wanting.
Do not criticize others until you have cleansed
yourself.

Sarcasm can cut as deeply as the sword.
Sensitivity blesses the recipient.

Each person is different from all others:
different thoughts,
different appearance,
different background,
different culture,
different politics,
different religion and
different beliefs.
Each is still a child of God.

Do not compare yourself with others.
Each person is uniquely made in God's own image.

Praise of others gives them a blessing.
Praise of yourself is foolish flattery.

The fool criticizes in public and praises in private.
The wise criticize in private and praise in public.

The fool's tongue gets him in trouble.
The wise speak with understanding and compassion.

The proud highlight their own virtues.
The wise celebrate the virtues of others.

The arrogant are quick to quarrel.
The wise are quick to seek peace.

Criticism is biased by the experience,
perspective and position of the critic.

It is far easier to find fault than to build anything.

The proud compare themselves
with others and feel superior.
The wise consider others and feel inadequate.

The arrogant associate with the wealthy,
the mighty and the powerful.
The wise walk with the poor, the meek and the lowly.

The arrogant act as if they are better than others.
The wise see others for their virtues,
not their deficiencies.

Do not find fault in others.
Celebrate their strengths instead.

Peace comes to those who care neither for
the praise of men nor the condemnation
and criticism of doubters.

The proud criticize their enemies.
The wise convert their enemies into friends.

The goals of the fool are power,
prestige, fame and fortune.
The goals of the wise are peace, joy, grace and love.

Criticism and Comparisons

"We want to avoid any criticism. . . .
For we are taking pains to do what is right,
not only in the eyes of the Lord
but also in the eyes of men."
2 Corinthians 8:20-21

"If anyone thinks he is something
when he is nothing, he deceives himself.
Each one should test his own actions.
Then he can take pride in himself,
without comparing himself to somebody else. . ."
Galatians 6:3-4

Discipline and Self-Control

Success is built upon discipline, commitment and focus. Every lesson learned, every improvement made, every vision realized, every goal met, every victory claimed rests upon the foundation of discipline and hard work. Freedom and discipline are necessary complements of each other. Without discipline, there can be no freedom.

"The fear of the Lord is the beginning of knowledge, but fools despise wisdom and discipline."

Proverbs 1:7

Likewise, there can be no discipline without self-control. Unless the tongue is controlled, there can be no song. Unless the mind is focused, there can be no learning. Unless our passions are kept in check, there can be no order. Without discipline and self-control, there can be no peace. When we are able to control our wants and desires, we find that the wants and desires cease to control us.

Discipline and self-control go together like love and romance. Where one is, the other is close at hand, but both are required to achieve wisdom.

Discipline is learned from adversity.
Growth comes through discipline.

Vision requires discipline.
Discipline enables vision to succeed.

Without risk, there is no progress.
Without discipline, risk is reckless.

The reckless throw caution to the wind.
The wise snatch caution from the wind.

The fool seeks freedom from discipline.
The wise find freedom in discipline.

The proud try to control others.
The wise control themselves.

The fool says, "Indulge thyself."
The fanatic says, "Deny thyself."
The wise partake in moderation.

Without discipline, true freedom cannot survive.
Without freedom, discipline is meaningless.

Natural ability may get you in the game.
Discipline keeps you in the game.

To the fool, good enough is acceptable.
To the wise, good enough is not good enough.

It is better to control your anger
than to command an army.
It is better to control your tongue
than to capture a treasure.

A quick temper causes pain.
Discipline is a mark of the wise.

The weak quit when first knocked down.
The wise get up and are not knocked out.

A man without discipline is a fool without substance.

You are not knocked out until you give up.
Discipline enables you to get back up.

Discipline and Self-Control

"The proverbs of Solomon, son of David, King of
Israel: for attaining wisdom and discipline;
for understanding words and insight;
for acquiring a discplined and prudent life,
doing what is right and just and fair; . . ."
Proverbs 1:1-3

"Whoever loves discipline loves knowledge,
but he who hates correction is stupid."
Proverbs 12:1

"He who guards his lips guards his life,
but he who speaks rashly will come to ruin."
Proverbs 13:3

". . . let us be self-controlled,
putting on faith and love as a breastplate,
and hope of salvation as a helmet."
1 Thessalonians 5:8

"Similarly, encourage the young men to be
self-controlled. In everything set them an example
by doing what is good. In your teaching, show
integrity, seriousness and soundness of speech. . . ."
Titus 2:6-8

"Be self-controlled and alert.
Your enemy the devil prowls around like a roaring lion
looking for someone to devour. Resist him. . . ."
1 Peter 5:8-9

There is a big difference between dreams and desires. Dreams are windows into our souls, visions of the possible, messages from the Divine. No species, other than human beings, is known to dream dreams. Desires which often accompany dreams can be positive longings for truth, honesty and wisdom, but often

> *"Delight yourself in the Lord and he will give you the desires of your heart."*
>
> Psalm 37:4

desires tend to be about illicit wants, pleasures, envy, greed and selfishness. Dreams can fuel new discoveries and profound spiritual experiences, while illicit desires can drive us into the depths of depression and depravity.

Dreams provide us with hope, inspiration, ambition and achievement beyond our wildest imagination. Dreams are an essential part of life as human beings. Dreaming itself is not dangerous. Failure to dream is. The danger is not that we dream too big. The danger is that our dreams are too small.

Consequently, we should encourage and pursue our dreams while we control and restrict our desires. Dream big and beyond the possible. Desire less to achieve significance.

Dreams forgotten are the seeds of discontentment.
Dreams pursued are the source of peace.

If you can dream it, you can do it.
Dreams are what reality can become.

Dreams are love letters from God
to guide your longings, to shape your desires
and to mold your essence.

Poverty is not the absence of things
but the craving for more.
Poverty is not having too little
but desiring too much.

The selfish pursue only their own desires.
The wise suppress their own desires to serve others.

The arrogant desire to satisfy only their own pleasures.
The wise seek God's pleasure.

The fool succumbs to his own desires.
The wise find joy in denying themselves.

The fool indulges temptation for self-gratification.
The wise reject temptation for divine affirmation.

The wicked trade purity for pleasure.
The wise reject pleasure for purity.

The fool trades permanent joy for temporary pleasure.
The wise seek perpetual peace.

The desire of the fool is to be respected by others.
The desire of the wise is to love others.

Dreams pursued at first seem impossible,
then improbable, then possible, then inevitable.
Do not let others spoil your dreams.

Dreams speak of the future,
while history speaks of the past.
The past is past, but dreams
provide hope for a better day.

Dreams are windows into the soul.
Desires are reflections of passion and pursuit.

Dreams provide the vision for hope and peace.
Desires provide the passion and discipline
to make the dreams come true.

Dreams are born of imagination and illusion,
but dreams bear hope and hope, peace.

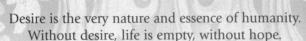

Desire is the very nature and essence of humanity.
Without desire, life is empty, without hope.

The desire of man is to live forever,
having produced a body of work and
deeds that have lasting purpose and meaning.

Desire feeds the soul with passion.
Passion gives life pleasure and purpose.

The greatest danger is not that we dream too big,
but that we do too little to make
our dreams come true.

Dreams and Desires

"What the wicked dreads will overtake him;
what the righteous desire will be granted."
Proverbs 10:24

"For I have the desire to do what is good,
but I cannot carry it out.
For what I do is not the good I want to do;
no, the evil I do not want to do—
this I keep on doing."
Romans 7:18-19

Faith and Hope

Hope involves anticipation with optimism and includes visualization of what is possible. But hope without faith is an empty vessel, like making a wish without believing it to be possible. Faith involves assurance that what is hoped for can and will come to pass.

> *"Though he slay me, yet will I hope in him. . . ."*
>
> Job 13:15

We exercise our faith daily. We do not know that electricity is connected to the light switch, but we have faith that the light will come on when we flip the switch. We cannot see the wind, but we know that wind will carry the seeds of all sorts of vegetation, enabling the forests to thrive, the flowers to bloom and the wheat to wave. Faith is the assurance of future probabilities, not just future possibilities. Faith involves believing when seeing is not possible. Faith overcomes doubt. Faith trumps pessimism. Faith conquers the faithless. Life without hope is pessimism personified, but life without faith is simply intolerable.

Hope reflects our desires. Faith reflects our dreams. Hope is passive. Faith is active. Faith builds hope, but hope without faith is fantasy.

A man without faith is a fool without hope.
Embrace faith, not despair.

Faith is being assured there is a way
when you cannot see a way.
Faith eliminates the uncertainty of survival.

Hope without faith is just wishful thinking.
Faith is hope in action.

Focus on faith.
What you focus on is what you get.

Expect the best.
Reject the rest.

Faith believes in what is not seen.
Faith rewards the believer.

Without faith, nothing is possible.
With faith, all things are possible.

Hope dreams of miracles.
Faith expects miracles.

An evil man destroys hope in others.
A good man gives hope to others.

Hope without faith is mere fantasy.
Faith without hope is a dream without a foundation.

Hope exudes optimism.
Faith secures positive results.

A goal without hope is like
a journey without a destination.

There can be no vision without hope.
There can be no victory without faith.

Hope is the idea of what is possible.
Faith is the belief in what is possible.

Hope is passive.
Faith is active.

Without faith, there is no hope.
Without hope, there are no miracles.
Without miracles, there is no faith.
Without faith, vision perishes.

Faith and Hope

"The righteous will live by faith."
Romans 1:17

"For it is by grace you have been saved, through faith—
and this not from yourselves, it is the gift of God—
not by works, so that no one can boast."
Ephesians 2:8-9

"Now faith is being sure of what we hope for
and certain of what we do not see."
Hebrews 11:1

"As the body without the spirit is dead,
so faith without deeds is dead."
James 2:26

Forgiveness runs completely counter to our human inclinations. When bad things happen to us because of the evil that others do, we want to respond in kind. We feel we need to fight back and to strike back in revenge in order to demonstrate that we are not soft, not pushovers, not someone to be taken lightly. Forgiving those who bring us harm makes us feel that somehow they have won.

". . . if my people, who are called by my name, will humble themselves and pray and seek my face and turn from their wicked ways, then will I hear from heaven and will forgive their sin and will heal their land."

2 Chronicles 7:14

Forgiveness does not let the wrong-doer off the hook; forgiveness deprives the evildoer of any hold on us. When we forgive another without any expectation of reward, we literally sense a burden lifted from us. While it is not natural to forgive, it is wise to do so. In forgiveness, we acknowledge our fundamental goodness, and we reap rewards that bring us peace. Forgiveness is a gift we give to those that harm and hurt us. In forgiveness, we offer true friendship.

Forgiveness is hard, but joy and peace are the products of forgiveness without expectation of reward.

Revenge is the work of the devil.
Forgiveness is the work of God.

Resentment never satisfies.
Forgiveness always satisfies.

Forgiveness frees the creditor as well as the debtor.
Forgiveness robs the debtor of his hold on the creditor.

The man with anger in his mouth
has no forgiveness in his heart.

Forgiveness is not found in the fool.
Mercy and compassion are traits of the wise.

Forgiveness is usually unfair,
but forgiveness frees.

Forgiveness gives a double blessing:
once to the one forgiven,
then to the one who forgives.

The wicked repay evil with evil.
The wise repay evil with forgiveness.

The fool is unwilling to forgive.
The wise refuse not to forgive.

Revenge seems to satisfy,
but forgiveness gives freedom to the forgiver.

Forgiveness is the first impulse of the Divine.

Forgive to live for God.
Forgive to receive from God.
Forgive to experience the grace and peace of God.

The fool never forgives his enemy.
The wise have many friends,
because the wise forgive.

Forgiveness is hard to do but worth the effort.
Forgiveness is a form of giving.

A forgiven enemy becomes your friend.
An unforgiven friend is a friend lost forever.

Forgive to live.
Live to forgive.

Forgiveness

"Therefore, if you are offering your gift at the altar and
there remember that your brother
has something against you,
leave your gift there in front of the altar.
First go and be reconciled to your brother;
then come and offer your gift."
Matthew 5:23-24

"Then Peter came to Jesus and asked,
'Lord, how many times shall I forgive my brother
when he sins against me?
Up to seven times?' Jesus answered,
'I tell you, not seven times, but seventy-seven times.'"
Matthew 18:21-22

"Be kind and compassionate to one another,
forgiving each other,
just as in Christ God forgave you."
Ephesians 4:32

"If we confess our sins,
he is faithful and just and will forgive us our sins
and purify us from all unrighteousness."
1 John 1:9

There is no substitute for true friends. There is a big difference between mere acquaintances and friends. Friends are there for you when you need them. Friends are there to help and heal you. They are there to protect and defend you. Friends make you stronger, tell you the truth when others lie, guide you when you are confused, hold you when you are lonely, listen to you when no one else will and protect you against the dangers of the night. Friends are friends forever.

"A man of many companions may come to ruin, but there is a friend who sticks closer than a brother."

Proverbs 18:24

Enemies are those who detest you, seek to hurt you, steal what is yours, spread gossip that damages your reputation and cheat against you. Many former friends turn against you for selfish reasons and become your enemy when they do. Friends turned enemies are the worst kind of enemy. True friends are precious gifts to be cherished. Enemies should be avoided but forgiven.

True friends are few and far between. Mere acquaintances and adversaries tend to be all around. There is great joy in true friendship. Cultivate true friendships with care.

A kind man has many friends.
An evil man has none.

Take issue with issues, not with people.
Take issue with policies, not with people.
Take issue with positions, not with people.

Look for the good in others.
They will strive to please you.

The fool hates his enemies.
The wise turn enemies into friends.

Loyal friends give you happiness. Things do not.
Relationships produce contentment. Things do not.

Pay attention to your enemies.
They will know about your weaknesses
and your mistakes.

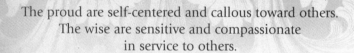

The proud are self-centered and callous toward others.
The wise are sensitive and compassionate
in service to others.

Betrayal of a friend lasts for a lifetime.
Forgiveness of an enemy builds bonds
that can last forever.

Flattery and friendship are opposites.
Flattery is a trap set by the fool.
Friendship is a gift offered by the wise.

An unforgiven friend becomes an enemy for life.
An enemy befriended becomes a friend forever.

Envy the wicked and you will join them.
Follow the wise and their wisdom will rub off.

The fool slanders his brother to gain the reward.
The wise praise their enemies to gain a brother.

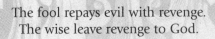

The fool repays evil with revenge.
The wise leave revenge to God.

The fool remembers the bad that others do
in order to get even with them.
The wise forget the evil that others do
in order to forgive and free them.

The fool learns from his own mistakes.
The wise learn from the mistakes of others.

The arrogant put down others to elevate themselves.
The wise put themselves down to elevate others.

The fool acts with an air of superiority.
The wise act with a sense of humility.

The wealthy cling to "mine and thine."
The wise embrace "you and yours."

The fool is arrogant and selfish.
The wise are humble and selfless.

The greedy are never content.
The wise are content and enjoy personal peace.

The frivolous laugh at others and make fun of them.
The wise laugh with others and have fun with them.

The fool seeks glory and praise.
The wise seek grace and peace.

The fool is a lone ranger.
The wise prosper in a village.

The fool compares his position
with others to feel important.
The wise use their position with others
to feel blessed.

The fool blames all but himself.
The wise praise all but themselves.

The selfish think of themselves first.
The wise think of others first.

The fool regards freedom as avoiding
the needs of others.
The wise find freedom in serving
the needs of others.

Friends and Enemies

"If your enemy is hungry, give him food to eat;
if he is thirsty, give him water to drink.
In doing this, you will heap burning coals on his head,
and the Lord will reward you."
Proverbs 25:21-22

"As iron sharpens iron,
so one man sharpens another."
Proverbs 27:17

"But I tell you who hear me: Love your enemies,
do good to those who hate you, bless those who
curse you, pray for those who mistreat you.
If someone strikes you on one cheek,
turn to him the other also.
If someone takes your cloak,
do not stop him from taking your tunic.
Give to everyone who asks you . . .
Do to others as you would have them do to you."
Luke 6:27-31

Generosity is a mark of wisdom and optimism. Those who experience the blessings of a gift affirm and praise the giver. Those who are the beneficiaries of a generous heart are blessed by the gift. Those who receive welcome the sincerity of a generous benefactor. Receiving is a blessing, but giving is a double blessing. Giving blesses the recipient as well as the giver.

> *"Give thanks to the Lord, for he is good; his love endures forever."*
>
> Psalm 118:1 and Psalm 136:1

Living a life of gratitude avoids the negative spirit of pessimism, transforms bitterness into blessings, cancels pride and selfishness and embraces the true purpose of life. Gratitude exudes a positive energy and brings joy to sadness and celebration to the ceremony. Living with a grateful heart assures a life of meaning, purpose, peace and joy. When we are truly thankful for what we have, we find contentment in what we have. Contentment gives us peace.

The spirit of gratitude is contagious and infectious. Where gratitude resides, joy, peace and happiness also reside.

A man who takes never has enough.
A man who gives is never without.

What we cling to we lose.
What we give away comes back to us multiplied.

One secret to living is giving.
You always get more than you give.

A stingy man is eager to become wealthy,
but soon his wealth is gone.
A generous man will never be without.

The wise give to live and live to give.

The greedy strive to get as much as
they can from as many as they can.
The wise strive to give as much as
they can to as many as they can.

The selfish pursue their own desires.
The wise pursue the needs of others.

Joy will find us if we are filled with gratitude.

The fool complains of having too little.
The wise are grateful for what they have.

The generosity of the wise blesses
the giver and the gift.
The fool stores his harvest in the silo
while the needy starve.

The proud fear losing their possessions.
The wise fear losing their souls.

The fool is never grateful, even for great favors.
The wise are always grateful, even for small blessings.

A miser takes to get.
The generous give without expectation of return.

A miser has problems because of his accumulations.
The wise get pleasure from gifts to others.

The greedy refuse to let go of what they have,
to gain what they desire.
Greed is not found in the wise.

Blessings cover the generous.
The stingy are broken and bruised.

A discerning mind without a generous heart is folly.
A generous heart combined with
a discerning mind leads to wisdom.

The wicked keep on getting.
The wise keep on giving.

The fool strives to get more.
The wise live to give more.

Giving is a double blessing.
The gift blesses the recipient and the giver.

Gratitude is easy to give.
It costs nothing. Its rewards are many.

Giving and Gratitude

"A generous man will prosper;
he who refreshes others will himself be refreshed."
Proverbs 11:25

"Give, and it will be given to you.
A good measure, pressed down, shaken together and
running over, will be poured into your lap.
For with the measure you use,
it will be measured to you."
Luke 6:38

"'It is more blessed to give than receive.'"
Acts 20:35

". . . give thanks in all circumstances,
for this is God's will for you in Christ Jesus."
1 Thessalonians 5:18

God and Spirit

God is the source of all that is good. God is the beginning of life and the end of existence. God is love, joy, hope, power, praise, peace and grace. God made all things, is in all things and gives meaning to all things. God is power and love, light and truth, hope and inspiration. Without God, nothing would be. With God, all things are possible.

> *"God said to Moses, 'I AM who I am. This is what you are to say to the Israelites: 'I AM has sent me to you.' . . . This is my name forever. . . .'"*
>
> Exodus 3:14-15

The Spirit of God is holy and sacred. The spirit of a man is his essence, his soul, his most unique quality. In spirit, man can hear the whisper of God. In spirit, man can feel the presence of God without being ashamed, afraid, angered or adorned. Man is both body and spirit. His body is physical, measured in time and space, but his essence is an infinite spirit, unlimited in time and in space.

God created man so that man would be in relationship with God. God wants us to offer our wonder, awe, praise and excitement to Him. When we do, God lets us enjoy His excitement and joy!

Love, hope, joy and peace are eternal gifts from God.
God loves you because He cannot help it. God is love.

Knowing about God is not knowing God.

Live for God's pleasure, not man's praise.
Live to give God pleasure,
not for your own enjoyment.

The unfaithful reject the life of the Spirit.
The wise embrace the spiritual quest of the soul.

Surrendering to God's will is the key to significance.
Seeking God's heart is the key to peace.
Striving for God's presence is the key to joy.

God does not always use the most qualified, but
God always qualifies the most available.

If you will let Him, God will turn
your messes into miracles,
your obstacles into opportunities,
your tests into triumphs,
your defeats into victories,
your pressures into poise,
your suffering into healing,
your hate into love, and
your death into life.

Unless God is involved in the answer,
there is no solution.

Unless God wants it done, do not do it.
Trust in God, not man.

Seek God's heart in all things.
Do God's will in all you do.

The foolish rely on their own power.
The wise trust in God's grace.

The proud are vain and profane.
The wise are pure and holy.

A spiritual foundation is essential to a significant life.
Cultivate the spiritual and significance will follow.

Many worship God because they are worried.
The wise surrender their worries to receive God's peace.

The fool pursues the passions of the flesh.
The wise seek the depths of the soul.

The selfish live solely for themselves.
The wise live to be instruments for God.

Expect God's miracles.
Accept God's blessings.

The fool causes messes.
The wise expect and accept God's miracles.

The skeptical do not believe in miracles.
The wise depend upon miracles.

Signs and wonders are evidence of God's assurance,
God's presence and God's grace.

The foolish pursue exterior things.
The wise seek internal peace.

The weak are content with their own strength.
The wise trust God's power and might.

The fool devotes his life to the pursuit of pleasure.
The wise find pleasure pursuing God's presence.

Security is illusive outside God's presence.
Security is assured under God's wings.

Things, honors and awards are fleeting.
God's presence is permanent.

The greatest wealth is found in God's pleasure.
The greatest joy comes from being in God's presence.

Heaven is a gift from God.
No one can ever
know enough,
earn enough,
save enough,
work enough,
risk enough,
give enough or
love enough
to merit a place in heaven.

The opposite of Spirit is matter.
Matter can be measured.
Matter has length, breadth, height and depth.
Spirit is freedom without form,
without shape, without a beginning or an end.

Evil is the Devil without the "D."

EGO means Edging God Out.

Character matters.
Humility matters.
Righteousness matters.
Integrity matters.
Service matters.
Truth matters.
CHRIST matters most.

The fool is too busy to pray.
The wise are too busy not to pray.

Natural ability is God's gift to you.
What you do with your ability
is your gift back to God.

Seek God's pleasure, not man's praise.
Seek God's blessing, not man's prestige.
Seek God's mercy, not man's judgment.

Strive to be in God's will, not in man's praise.
Strive to be in God's presence, not man's power.
Strive to be holy, not to be honored by man.

Without the lie, there would have been no accusation.
Without the accusation,
there would have been no trial.
Without the trial,
there would have been no conviction.
Without the conviction,
there would have been no cross.
Without the cross, there would be no promise.
Without the promise,
there would be no hope of life eternal.

Without God, there is no healing.
Without God, there is no mercy.

Without God, there is no power.
Without God, there is no pleasure.

Without God, there is no meaning.
Without God, there is no significance.

Without God, there is no understanding.
Without God, there is no wisdom.

Without God, there is no faith.
Without God, there is no victory.

Without God, there is no purpose.
Without God, there is no peace.

Without God, there is no hope.
Without God, there is no joy.
Without God, there is no love.

Without God, there is no Truth.
Without God, there is no Way.
Without God, there is no Life.

God and Spirit

"And now, O Israel, what does the
Lord your God ask of you
but to fear the Lord your God, to walk in all his ways,
to love him, to serve the Lord your God
with all your heart and with all your soul,
and to observe the Lord's commands and decrees
that I am giving you today for your own good?"
Deuteronomy 10:12-13

"I trust in God's unfailing love for ever and ever."
Psalm 52:8

"Know that the Lord is God. It is he who made us,
And . . . we are his people, the sheep of his pasture . . .
For the Lord is good and his love endures forever;
his faithfulness continues through all generations."
Psalm 100:3,5

Most of us desire to have a life filled with pleasure. Pleasure can be another word for party. Pleasure certainly includes partying, but pleasure includes much, much more. Pleasure comes from satisfying our senses, from feeding our feelings and emotions. Pleasure can be the direct result of doing good for others, but pleasure can also occur at the expense and to the detriment of others or as a result of the evil we do or we think.

> *"Where were you when I laid the earth's foundation? . . . who laid its cornerstone—while the morning stars sang together and all the angels shouted for joy?"*
>
> Job 38:4,6-7

Sensual pleasures, victorious pleasures and emotional pleasures can be very satisfying, but true joy comes only from being in the presence of God. Joy is the very fragrance of God's grace. True joy comes to those who feel God's touch, sense His presence and embrace His pleasure.

We seek a life full of pleasure, but true joy is what we most desire. True joy is found in seeking God and in serving others. True joy is found in knowing God's will and doing it. True joy is desired above gold and silver.

Fame is gain for an instant.
Joy is pleasure forever.

Pleasure is temporary.
Joy is eternal.

Joy comes through God's presence,
not from man's power, prestige or possessions.

Pleasure comes from feeling and touching.
Joy comes from knowing and believing.

Joy emanates from the heart and the soul,
not from the eyes and the hands.

The fool is pessimistic.
The wise exude joy.

Joy is the sweetest fruit of the Spirit.
Where joy is there also is the presence of God.

Feasting and frivolity follow the fool.
Joy and compassion are traits of the wise.

The wise reject the pleasure of things
in favor of the joy of wisdom.

Rewards are many to the proud,
but joy is sufficient for the wise.

JOY comes when we live life in this priority:
Jesus first, Others second, Yourself last.

Joy comes not from the abundance of things
but from the absence of things.

Joy is not found in the pursuit of pleasure.
Joy comes from being in God's will.

Happiness for the fool comes
from accumulating things.
Joy for the wise comes from gratitude,
laughter and love of others.

The fool desires to live a life
with abundance and pleasure.
The wise desire to live a life of significance and joy.

Joy is found along the journey of life,
not just at the end of it.

Joy comes not from seeking happiness,
but from teaching others,
serving others, giving to others,
sharing with others and loving others.

Joy is found in the twinkle of a child's eyes
and in the wonder of a child's innocence.

Joy retained is joy diminished.
Joy shared is joy multiplied.

Joy is an attitude to be lived,
not an event to be anticipated.

Wherever possible, let your joy be complete.
Demonstrate your cheerfulness, excitement, passion
and pleasure. Do not let pessimissism dull your joy.

The principal enemies of joy are
pride, selfishness and arrogance.

Joy is a choice to be made,
not a gift to be received or a thing to be grasped.
Joy comes to those who choose it.

A joyful life is found in someone to love,
something worthy to do,
some meaningful service for others to give.

Blessed are the joyful,
for they shall receive the joy
they have given to others.

Joy and Pleasure

"A fool finds pleasure in evil conduct,
but a man of understanding delights in wisdom."
Proverbs 10:23

"The prospect of the righteous is joy,
but the hopes of the wicked come to nothing."
Proverbs 10:28

"If you obey my commands,
you will remain in my love,
just as I have obeyed my Father's
commands and remain in his love.
I have told you this so that my joy may be in you
and that your joy may be complete."
John 15:10-11

"If you have any encouragement
from being united with Christ,
if any comfort from his love,
if any fellowship with the Spirit,
if any tenderness and compassion,
then make my joy complete
by being like-minded, having the same love,
being one in spirit and purpose."
Philippians 2:1-2

Kindness, Compassion and Mercy

Being kind, compassionate and merciful costs very little, but the rewards can be enormous. People who are kind, who show others empathy and compassion and who demonstrate mercy for others are welcomed servants, counselors, consolers and healers. They exude a genuine sense of caring and an honest feeling of concern. They demonstrate humanity at its best. They are self-assured, comfortable and humble. They are people who attract others like a magnet.

*"And what does the Lord require of you?
To act justly and to love mercy and to walk humbly with your God."*

Micah 6:8

Kindness is the opposite of revenge, anger and rage. Compassion is the opposite of arrogance, pride and selfishness. Mercy embodies the strength of caring and the power of genuine concern. These qualities are fruits of the human spirit and some of the best of humanity. Our kindness, compassion and mercy are forever our gifts back to God, but they are also a reflecttion of our attitude of joy, gratitude and peace toward others. These are the ingredients of a life of significance.

Kindness costs nothing but gains much.

Kindness and gentleness are qualities of a soul at peace. The cornerstone of goodness is compassion.

The fool wants revenge.
The wise demonstrate compassion and mercy.

Compassion is at the heart and soul of the wise.
Revenge and retribution are weapons of the fool.

Justice is the cry of the fool.
Mercy is the plea of the wise.

An act done with a sense of duty will be soon forgotten. An act of kindness done without an expectation of any return will be remembered forever.

The robes of the fool are pride and self-interest.
The cloak of the wise covers acts
of compassion and kindness.

The heart of compassion is caring,
without expectation of reward or recognition.

The weak reject mercy as the absence of power.
The wise embrace mercy and kindness
as a reflection of their power.

Kindness is a weakness to the wicked
but a strength of the wise.

Happiness and peace are the product of
a life filled with kindness and compassion.

The courage to show compassion for
the weak, the poor and the disadvantaged
is found in daring to care for others.

The powerful condemn the guilty.
The condemned beg for mercy.
The wise demonstrate compassion and kindness.

Random acts of kindness may seem small to the kind,
but they change the world of the recipient.

Kindness seeks not to be rewarded,
but to renew and refresh others.
Kindness has its own rewards.

Mercy is thought by some to be a sign of weakness.
Instead, mercy is a sign of compassion
and kindness of the strong.

Compassion is grace without
criticism or condemnation.

Kindness is found in a simple smile,
an encouraging word, an expression of affirmation
and an act of compassion.

Never pass up a chance to say a kind word,
to share a kind thought and to do a kind thing.

There is no such thing as a small act of kindness.
Kindness brings its own sunshine and its own rewards.

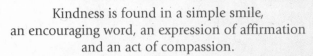

The greatest gift of God to man is the gift to choose.
The greatest gift of man to God is
choosing to serve others with care and compassion.

Kindness, Compassion and Mercy

"But love your enemies, do good to them, and lend
to them without expecting to get anything back.
Then your reward will be great,
and you will be sons of the Most High,
because he is kind to the ungrateful and wicked.
Be merciful, just as your Father is merciful."
Luke 6:35-36

"But the fruit of the Spirit is love, joy, peace,
patience, kindness, goodness, faithfulness,
gentleness and self-control.
Against such things there is no law."
Galatians 5:22-23

"Get rid of all bitterness, rage and anger, brawling
and slander, along with every form of malice.
Be kind and compassionate to one another, forgiving
each other, just as in Christ God forgave you."
Ephesians 4:31-32

Leadership and Character

Leadership and character are qualities always found together. Leadership embodies the qualities that define what character means: honesty, integrity, perseverance, commitment, affirmation and endurance. Leaders inspire others, motivate others, encourage others, praise others, care about others. Leaders are available to take bold steps, to move against the grain, to chart the unknown, to press on for the prize.

> *"Lead me,*
> *O Lord, in your*
> *righteousness*
> *because of my*
> *enemies—*
> *make straight your*
> *way before me."*
>
> Psalm 5:8

It is not possible to be an effective leader without being a person of high moral and ethical values. Followers do not follow one who is not willing to step forward, to speak up and to expect more than the followers can muster on their own. Without inspiration based upon personal integrity and internal honesty, a person will not be trusted to lead.

Some men lead because they have power and position to control, to punish, to condemn. People follow them out of fear, because they have to. True leaders demonstrate character, principle and wisdom. People follow them out of admiration, inclination and inspiration. They follow true leaders because they want to, not because they have to.

Motivation is not enough for leadership.
Leadership requires perspiration as well as inspiration.

The fool leads his followers from behind.
The wise lead by example from the front.

Every leader is a reader.
Not every reader is a leader.

The righteous pursue the path of honor.
The fool is stuck in the gutter of forgotten fame.

Scorn and distrust follow the fool.
Respect and honor greet the wise.

The ABCs of effective leadership are:
Availability,
Boldness and
Character.

Appreciation, affirmation and approval
are the tools of leadership.
They are tangible evidence of the value of others.

The fool waits to complete his "to do list"
when he has more time.
The wise understand that there is never
"more time" than now.

It is said of the proud, "Well said."
It is said of the wise, "Well done."

A wise leader can save a nation.
Conflict without victory follows the fool.

Fire refines iron into steel.
Leaders are shaped by overcoming opposition.

A man without character is a ship
without a rudder.
A leader without integrity is a fool
without a following.

The wicked trade character and integrity for prestige.
The wise measure prestige by character and integrity.

The proud make excuses for their mistakes.
The wise accept responsibility for their mistakes.

Character is a virtue in and of itself.
Character reflects the essence of the soul.

Honors are easier to win than honor is to live.
Honor follows character, integrity and wisdom.

The wise favor honor over honors,
truth over treasures and peace over prizes.

A righteous life is better with little
than a life of selfish pride filled with many rewards.

There is honor among the righteous,
but none among the wicked.

Integrity matters.
Right matters.
Truth matters.
Character matters.

The corrupt do not honor integrity.
The wise rely on their integrity.

Leaders affirm others.

Leadership embodies character and integrity.

A life committed to honesty and integrity
rejects most temptations before they arise.

Live so that your life carves
an epithet of character, integrity and honesty.

Live so that your steps are not
footprints in the sands of time,
but are words and deeds written
in the hearts of those you serve.

Extraordinary ability, superior intelligence
and Olympic achievement are hollow
without honor, character and integrity.

There can be no book of wisdom without
chapters on character, honesty, truth and integrity.

Treat a man with respect,
and he will work hard to meet your expectations.

Leadership and Character

"In your unfailing love you will lead the people
you have redeemed. In your strength you
will guide them to your holy dwelling. . . ."
Exodus 15:13

"Show me your ways, O Lord, teach me your paths;
guide me in your truth and teach me,
for you are God my Savior,
and my hope is in you all day long."
Psalm 25:4-5

"The fear of the Lord leads to life:
Then one rests content, untouched by trouble."
Proverbs 19:23

". . . we also rejoice in our sufferings, because
we know that suffering produces perservance;
perservance, charcter; and character, hope."
Romans 5:3-4

"Therefore, as God's chosen people, holy and
dearly loved, clothe yourselves with compassion,
kindness, humility, gentleness and patience."
Colossians 3:12

No two emotions are more polar opposites than love and hate, yet often one turns into the other. Love and hate involve intense but opposite emotions. Love is positive, while hate is negative. Love cares, while hate rejects. Love embraces, while hate backs away. Love is good, while hate is evil. Love is patient and kind, while hate is impatient and angry. Love feels, touches, embraces and excites, while hate repels and rejects. Love is the highest point on the mountain, while hate is the lowest depth of the pit.

> *"Through love and faithfulness sin is atoned for; through the fear of the Lord a man avoids evil."*
>
> Proverbs 16:6

Love can turn into hate through betrayal, dishonesty, gossip and broken promises. Hate can turn into love through kindness, forgiveness and compassion. The single biggest key to living a life of peace and joy is love.

Therefore, choose to love others in all circumstances, so that your wisdom in loving becomes a truth in their living.

Do not love for the glory of life.
Live for the glory of love.

The proud surrender their lives
to the love of power.
The wise surrender their lives
to the power of love.

The man who stops loving stops living.
A person without love is a fool without purpose.

Never hate anything but hate.
We begin to die when we begin to hate.

Hate is a four-letter word grounded in fear.
Hate corrodes the container in which it resides.
Hope is a four-letter word based on love.
Love is a four-letter word describing God.

In love, our differences disappear.
In love, there is no self, just the other.

The selfish love only those who love them.
The wise love others for who they are,
not what they do.

Hate destroys the one who hates and
gives power to the one hated.
Love empowers the one who loves
and the one who is loved.

Hate has no remedy except forgiveness and love.
Hate infects the hater with a terminal malady.

Love is the essence of living.
Without love, there is no life.

Love is more than feelings,
more than pleasure, more than joy.
Love is the very soul of being human,
the water and air of life itself.

Love endures, embraces, understands,
accepts, forgets and forgives.

Love is infused in all laws that last.
Without love, law cannot endure.

Love is the mystery that gives life
meaning, purpose, power and soul.

Hate destroys.
Love builds up.

Hate will turn upon itself.
Love always turns outward to others.

Hate destroys.
Love is the remedy for hate.

Love of self is love defeating.
Love of others is love revealing.

Love of self is the cruelest malady.
Love cannot abide where there is selfish pride.

If you have love of another,
you need nothing else.
If you do not have love of another,
nothing else much matters.

Love enchants, inspires, creates and gives meaning
to everything it touches.

What man desires is love, not pleasure.

Love is the fuel that drives destiny.

Hate poisons and corrupts all it touches. Love gives
birth to compassion, mercy, grace, and peace.

Love like there is no tomorrow.
Love not given away results is
a life not lived in love.

Live to love!
Do not love to live.

Love and Hate

"You love righteousness and hate wickedness;
therefore God, your God, has set you above
companions by annointing you with the oil of joy."
Psalm 45:7

"There are six things the Lord hates, seven that
are detestable to him: haughty eyes, a lying tongue,
hands that shed innocent blood, a heart that devises
wicked schemes, feet that are quick to rush into evil,
a false witness who pours out lies and a man
who stirs up dissension among brothers."
Proverbs 6:16-19

"Hate evil, love good. . . ."
Amos 5:15

"Love must be sincere. Hate what is evil;
cling to what is good.
Be devoted to one another in brotherly love.
Honor one another above yourselves . . .
Be joyful in hope, patient in affliction,
faithful in prayer. . . . Practice hospitality."
Romans 12:9-10,12-13

"Love is patient, love is kind. It does not envy,
it does not boast, it is not proud. It is not rude,
it is not self-seeking, it is not easily angered,
it keeps no record of wrongs.
Love does not delight in evil but
rejoices with the truth.
It always protects, always trusts,
always hopes, always perseveres.
Love never fails. . . . And now these three remain:
faith, hope and love. But the greatest of these is love."
1 Corinthians 13:4-8,13

A principal driving force in our lives is the quest for more money and more things. We incorrectly believe that our lives will be happier, our families will be healthier and our jobs will be more fulfilling if only we had more money. More money means to many people more prestige, success and importance. We think that the more we have the easier life will be, the greater security we will enjoy and the less stress we will encounter. The opposite is generally true.

> *"Whoever loves money never has money enough; whoever loves wealth is never satisfied with his income. This too is meaningless."*
>
> Ecclesiastes 5:10

In truth we have too much stuff. Our stuff actually gets in our way. More things block our path to solitude, joy, peace and spirit. Significance comes not from bigger, faster, more expensive stuff, but rather from divesting ourselves of our thirst for more and finding ways to share with others what we have. When we lose our insatiable appetites for more stuff and substitute a sincere desire to serve others, we find the path to peace, joy and grace.

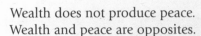

Wealth does not produce peace.
Wealth and peace are opposites.

Wealth hoards more.
Peace surrenders more.

The wise seek knowledge not power,
understanding not possessions,
wisdom not money.

The fool purchases things he does not need
with money he does not have
to impress people he does not even know.

The wealthy trust in their money, power and fame.
The wise trust in God's grace,
God's peace and God's presence.

Prosperity without honor is like life without joy.

Accumulation of more things
deprives man of the most important things.
The most important things in life are not things at all.

Money is not the source of evil.
The love of money is.

The rich seek more money.
The wise are content with less.

The rich yearn for more money.
The wise regard money as a necessary evil.

The rich acquire in abundance.
The wise give in abundance.

The wealthy feel secure with their
money, power and possessions.
To the wise, security comes from knowledge,
understanding and wisdom.

The fool spends his life making a living.
The wise devote themselves to making a life.

Prosperity nudges the fool away from God.
Prosperity humbles the wise.

Power used against the weak is bullying.
Power used for the weak is the foundation of peace.
Power is best used when not used at all.

Power, wealth, prestige and fame are temporary.
Grace, peace, joy and love are permanent.

The fool is rich in earthly things.
The wise are rich in spiritual virtues.

Satisfaction to the fool is found in things.
The wise know that things do not satisfy.

The man that runs on the road of accumulation
never reaches the finish line.

The fool holds on tightly to what he has.
The wise share generously what they have.

The fool measures his greatness
by the quantity of his possessions.
The wise measure their significance
by the quality of their compassion.

Money breeds discontent and distrust.

Money as a tool is neutral.
Money can either be used for evil or for good.
Use it wisely.

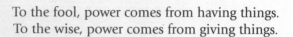

To the fool, power comes from having things.
To the wise, power comes from giving things.

Money can buy a house but not a home.
Money can buy a clock but not time.

Money can buy a bed but not sleep.
Money can buy a title but not respect.

Money can buy fun but not joy.
Money can buy things but not peace.

Money can buy sex but not love.
Money can buy pleasure but not joy.

Money can buy medicine but not health.
Money can buy a smile but not happiness.

Money can buy possessions but not peace.
Money can buy companionship but not friendship.

Money can buy rewards but not respect.
Money can buy a victory but not honor.

Money can buy a library but not knowledge.
Money can buy experience but not wisdom.

Money and Things

"Moreover, when God gives any man
wealth and possessions
and enables him to enjoy them,
to accept his lot and be happy in his work—
this is a gift of God."
Ecclesiastes 5:19

"No one can serve two masters.
Either he will hate the one and love the other, or
he will be devoted to the one and despise the other.
You cannot serve both God and Money."
Matthew 6:24

"For the love of money is a root of
all kinds of evil. . . ."
1 Timothy 6:10

"Be shepherds of God's flock that is under
your care, . . . not greedy for money,
but eager to serve; . . ."
1 Peter 5:2

Past, Present and Future

The past is where we have come from, and the future is where we are going, but the present is where we reside. The past has shaped our thoughts through experience. It is not possible nor is it even desirable to shed all remnants of the past. There is no substitute for experience, and experience is just another way of saying the past. But too much emphasis on the past will pollute the present and restrict the future. We need to learn the lessons of the past without letting our past experiences completely dominate our present.

". . . there is a future for the man of peace. But all sinners will be destroyed; the future of the wicked will be cut off."

Psalm 37:37-38

Likewise, the future is not yet here, nor is it ever knowable. As much as we might want to predict with certainty what will happen, the future will always be a mystery. What we have for sure is today, right now, the eternal present. If we make the best of this very moment, our past and our future will take care of themselves. The past is past! The future is a mystery. Right now is a gift. That is why now is called the present.

Your yesterdays tomorrow will be
what you are doing now.

The fool spends for today.
The wise build bridges for tomorrow.

Worship of the past pollutes the
present and corrupts the future.
Understanding the past can
avoid mistakes in the present.

Now is never before.
Now will never be again.

The fool basks in the light of his past glories.
The wise focus on present conditions
and future opportunities.

The young are always getting ready to live.
The wise cherish each present moment for what it is.

The fool dwells in the past.
The wise use the past to shape the future.

The lazy put off until tomorrow what is needed to be
done today. The wise do now what today requires.

The proud look back to relive their past glories.
The wise look inward to live a life
of future significance.

This very moment is pregnant with possibilities.
Be ready to seize this moment and
suck the marrow out of each instance.

As for the past, no tears.
As for the present, cheers.
As for the future, no fears.

All we have in this life is the eternal now.
Use it or lose it.

History is a good teacher.
To understand today,
you must first understand the past.

Focus not on what has been,
but instead on what can be.

Yesterday is always present.
Tomorrow never seems to come.

A life of "if only" leaves
the present tainted by the past.

The past is past.
The future is perfect.

The past is not responsible for your present.
There are no rewinds, returns, reviews or instant
replays. The past is over. Focus on the present.

Seize the moment and savor it completely.
This present moment will never be again.

Past, Present and Future

"Forget the former things;
do not dwell on the past."
Isaiah 43:18

"In the beginning was the Word, and the Word was
with God, and the Word was God. He was with God in
the beginning. Through him all things were made;
without him nothing was made that has been made.
In him was life, and that life was the light of men."
John 1:1-4

"I consider that our present sufferings are not worth
comparing with the glory that will be revealed in us."
Romans 8:18

Patience is a sign of wisdom, an assurance that all good things happen in due course. For the go-getter, patience is hard, because we want the spoils of victory, and we want them now. Patience is not a natural human characteristic, because we tend to want what we want, and we do not want to wait to get it. Patience comes with experience, and patience reflects the wisdom that comes from learning the lessons of having pushed too hard in the past.

> *"Great peace have they who love your law, and nothing can make them stumble."*
>
> Psalm 119:165

Peace and poise are also visible signs of the wisdom that comes through experience. Two of the fruits of spiritual life are patience and peace. Poise comes when we take a deep breath and surrender to the beauty that is before us. Poise is a natural result of the confidence and assurance that flow from being at peace.

When hurried, pressed and anxious, take a deep breath. Pause to reflect poise, and peace will invade your spirit.

Hurry is an enemy of peace.
Patience may be God's wisest work.

Peace is being content with what you have
and being satisfied with who you are.

Patience rewards the pursuer.
Pursue peace with passion.

Patience produces confidence, control and peace.
Stress, anxiety and lack of control
are the signs of impatience.

Avoid conflict through patience.
Peace is more than the absence of conflict.

Pride thrives on conflict.
Patience avoids conflict.

The proud are stubborn and arrogant.
The wise are patient and kind.

Sleep comes easily to the wise.
The wicked cannot sleep because of their guilt.

Guilt poisons the days of the corrupt.
Peace fills the life of the wise.

The nervous tremble under pressure.
The wise turn pressure into poise.

The critical stir up trouble and discontentment.
The wise seek peace and harmony.

Peace is found in love and forgiveness,
not in power and possessions.

The wise seek grace, mercy, peace and joy.
The arrogant seek power, position,
prestige and possessions.

The man with a pure heart and
a quiet spirit has treasures in heaven.
Turmoil, conflict and disruption follow the fool.

Practice poise to achieve peace.
Patience is worth the wait.

The fool demands immediate results.
Patience is a mark of the wise.

The peace that passes understanding comes from faith.
Patience and poise also rest on faith.

Now is where you live.
The past is gone and will never return.

The future is what will happen
in a second or a century.
Now is here, but now is illusive,
fleeting and all we have.

The fruits of patience are eternal.
The product of haste is waste.

Patience mediates the passions of discord,
distrust and deceit.
Patience holds the seeds of hope.

Patience and wisdom are brothers.

Simplify, slow down and have patience.

One way to have a peaceful life is to
enjoy the awesome wonder and
majesty of God's presence.

Peace comes to those that wait.
Obedience is the key to peace. Integrity matters.
Surrender to be free. Expect a miracle..

Choose the peace of God,
not the praise from men.

Patience, Peace and Poise

"Turn from evil and do good;
seek peace and pursue it."
Psalm 34:14

"A patient man has great understanding,
but a quick-tempered man displays folly."
Proverbs 14:29

"A man's wisdom gives him patience;
it is to his glory to overlook an offense."
Proverbs 19:11

"Peace I leave with you;
my peace I give to you."
John 14:27

"But the fruit of the Spirit is love, joy, peace,
patience, kindness, goodness, faithfulness,
gentleness and self-control.
Against such things there is no law."
Galatians 5:22-23

Pride and Humility

Pride, arrogance and selfishness are qualities that are uniquely human. We strut our honors, achievements and victories as if we were the sole architect of those results. We deceive ourselves into believing that we are superior to others, because we succeed in winning the game, getting the job, being selected for the honor. In truth, pride gets in the way of wisdom, because humility, not pride, is the mark of the wise.

> *"I hate pride and arrogance,*
> *evil behavior and perverse speech."*
>
> Proverbs 8:13

We do not accomplish any achievement without the help of teachers, coaches, consultants, advisors, friends, family and faith. We are not alone, and our accomplishments are reflections of the collective efforts of all those from whom we have received support. Everything we dream, visualize, think and believe is a direct and indirect result of the efforts of those who have gone before us. We are not entitled to be proud because of our efforts. We should, instead, reflect humility, because we are part of the tapestry of past thoughts and achievements of others. Humility comes from the lessons of experience.

Hypocrisy is the companion of the fool.
Humility is the companion of the wise.

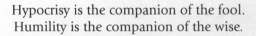

Greatness among men is the goal of the fool.
Humility before God is the desire of the wise.

A man filled with pride has a lot of company.
A humble man travels the high road
without much traffic.

Pride, arrogance and selfishness are
the major sins that block a peaceful and joyful life.

Pride repels.
Humility attracts.

Bigotry and arrogance accompany the wicked.
The wise enjoy blessings from many.

Pride and arrogance clutter the mind of the fool.
Humility is the mark of the wise.

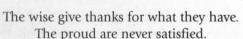

The wise give thanks for what they have.
The proud are never satisfied.

There is no peace for those filled with arrogance.
Pride blocks our path to God.

Pride pollutes the joys of life.
Wisdom is like a fresh mountain spring.

Boasting puts others down.
Humility elevates others above self.

The fool is selfish.
The wise are selfless.

The proud work to hear the applause of man.
The humble listen for the affirmation of God.

The fool knows no humility.
The wise are known for their humility.

Pride and Humility

"He guides the humble in what is right and
teaches them his way."
Psalm 25:9

"When pride comes, then comes disgrace,
but with humility comes wisdom."
Proverbs 11:2

"Pride goes before destruction,
a haughty spirit before a fall."
Proverbs 16:18

"For whoever exalts himself will be humbled,
and whoever humbles himself will be exalted."
Matthew 23:12

"Be completely humble and gentle;
be patient, bearing with one another in love."
Ephesians 4:2

"All of you, clothe yourselves with
humility toward one another,
because, 'God opposes the proud but
gives grace to the humble.'"
1 Peter 5:5

Most of the time, what is right and what is wrong are clearly defined. Hurting another to gain a reward is not right. Taking what belongs to another without fair compensation is wrong. Distinguishing between what is right and wrong is usually not hard to do. Sometimes, however, making the right choice is difficult. The consequences of our proposed action are not clear. The impact our decisions will have on others may not be easily understood. The future is blurry, uncertain and mysterious.

> *"The law of the Lord is perfect, reviving the soul. The statutes of the Lord are trustworthy, making wise the simple. The precepts of the Lord are right, giving joy to the heart. . . ."*
>
> Psalm 19:7-8

There are many tools for measuring what is right and what is wrong. This collection of timeless thoughts and truths is one example. What does the most good for the most people is one example. What does the least harm for the greatest number of people is another standard for discerning right from wrong. A positive role model, an honest example, a caring mentor, a terrific father often provide guides for future action. Would my father approve? Would I be proud or ashamed to tell others what I am contemplating doing? Perhaps the best tool is the small voice within us which knows our intent, our purpose and our motive. That voice is sometimes called God within us. Follow that voice.

Power and right are different.
Power does not make doing anything right.

The lazy look for the easy way.
The wise look for the right way.

A man who runs on the wrong path
will never reach the right goal.

A deed done to hurt another
cannot ever be done for the right reason.

Better to live a life of poverty
than to live a life of moral corruption.

Doing what is right, especially when unpopular,
reflects the wisdom of the wise.

Fame lasts for a moment.
Righteousness lasts a lifetime.

The path of the righteous is littered with obstacles
which the fool chooses to embrace
but the righteous reject.

The wise choose the road of moral correctness.
The corrupt associate with moral decay.

Lies and corruption are like peas in a pod.
Where one is, the other is close by.

Moral clarity guides the righteous.
Moral decay burdens the wicked.

Do what you do because it is right,
not because it is popular.

Integrity is what you do
when no one is watching,
and there is no chance of getting caught.

Be consistently true to yourself and to your word.

Avoid taking anything negative as
being directed at you personally.
Avoid making assumptions and speculating.

The life of the fool will be short and difficult.
The life of the righteous will be
filled with joy and peace.

Cherish treasures and die poor.
Stand for truth and live with God forever.

There is no right way to do a wrong thing.
There is no worth in achieving an unworthy task.

Wrong is wrong, no matter who says differently.
Right is right, no matter how many people disagree.

Widely held wrong opinions are still wrong opinions.
Facts are still facts, even if everyone ignores them.

Wrong is not a matter of opinion,
belief, understanding or culture.
Right is not a matter of opinion,
belief, understanding or culture.

A bully pushes his power upon others.
The wise use their influence for the benefit of others.

The corrupt are morally perverse.
The wise are morally upright.

The wicked repay good with evil.
The righteous do what is right,
even when it is not popular.

Knowing right from wrong is not enough.
Doing what is right is what counts.

If you do not have time to do it right,
when will you have time to do it over?

The wicked are despised.
The righteous are honored.

The weak go along to get along.
The wise stand steadfastly for what is right.

The naive leave conscience for tomorrow.
The wise embrace conscience
every moment of every day.

Vengeance cries "an eye for an eye."
Wisdom knows that "an eye for an eye"
leads to blindness.

The corrupt travel a crooked road of moral decay.
The wise travel the straight road of righteousness.

The fool is often wrong and never in doubt.
The wise do what is right and never look back.

Revere the righteous.
Reject the wretched.

Doing wrong never results in a right result.
Doing wrong, even for a good reason, is still wrong.

Doing wrong spoils the spoils.
Doing wrong never is right.

Right and Wrong

"There is a way that seems right to a man,
but in the end it leads to death."
Proverbs 14:12

"Finally, brothers, whatever is true, whatever is noble,
whatever is right, whatever is pure,
whatever is lovely, whatever is admirable—
if anything is excellent or praiseworthy—
think about such things."
Philippians 4:8

"And as for you, brothers,
never tire of doing what is right."
2 Thessalonians 3:13

Every human endeavor involves risk. Risks always accompany change, and change always results in anxiety. Anxiety is the opposite of poise. To accomplish anything, there are obstacles to overcome and challenges to meet. Whether, when and how those difficulties are resolved involves uncertainty, and that uncertainty produces tension, tension causes stress and stress results in anxiety. Without risk, however, nothing would ever be accomplished.

> *"The ordinances of the Lord are sure and altogether righteous . . . in keeping them there is great reward."*
>
> Psalm 19:9,11

The greatest rewards come when we overcome the greatest challenges. Fear not that your dreams involve great risk. Fear instead that your dreams do not risk enough, that we dream too small, that we dare too little, that our goals are too low. Dare to be great in deeds and in humility.

Great risk often involves great reward, but great risk can also involve great failure. Risk wisely, so that your rewards may be worthy but also wise.

View risk as an opportunity for achievement,
not as a danger to be avoided.

Three keys to significant living are:
Risk more, give more and love more.

Change involves risk.
Uncertainty accompanies risk.
Movement embodies both risk and uncertainty.

A ship is safe in the harbor,
but ships were made to sail the seas.

All of the achievements of man
were once only a dream, a fantasy, an impossibility.
Without risk, nothing would ever be accomplished.

It is far better to try and fail than to fail to try.
You cannot discover a new thing
without doing a thing a new way.

There is no advancement without movement.
There is no movement without risk.

Risk not, gain not.

Without the risk, there is no reward.
Without trying, there is no victory.

No mistakes mean no discoveries.
No failures mean no attempts.

The fool avoids risks in pursuit of security.
The wise overcome risks to achieve peace.

Fear of the unknown is common.
Overcoming fear of uncertainty is
what the journey of life is all about.

Risk is inherent in all endeavors.
Without risk, life would be dull indeed.

The greatest risks do not always
produce the greatest rewards.
But if there is no risk, there can be no reward.

Courage is not the absence of fear.
Courage is moving forward in the face of fear.

Be bold in the face of uncertainty.
Risk cautiously. Dare mightily.

Risks and Rewards

"He who is kind to the poor lends to the Lord,
and he will reward him for what he has done."
Proverbs 19:17

"The wicked man flees though no one pursues,
but the righteous are as bold as a lion."
Proverbs 28:1

"I the Lord search the heart and examine the mind,
to reward a man according to his conduct,
according to what his deeds deserve."
Jeremiah 17:10

"For God did not give us a spirit of timidity,
but a spirit of power, of love and of self-discipline."
2 Timothy 1:7

Living a life of service is living a life of significance. Those that serve the needs of others are twice blessed: The one served is blessed by the service rendered, and the one who serves gets the joy of being the servant. Service rendered for others becomes a gift of gratitude, a deed done with empathy and caring, an opportunity to make a positive difference in the life of another. Service is an act of selflessness.

> *"Instead, whoever wants to become great among you must be your servant, and whoever wants to be first must be your slave— just as the Son of Man did not come to be served, but to serve . . ."*
>
> Matthew 20:26-28

The wise are servants for the benefit of others. Service for others becomes the outward expression of the inward love of the Divine. Those who want to be served by others are arrogant and selfish, while those who render service for others are humble and selfless. Service means doing something for the benefit of others. Service is active not passive. The foundational path to peace and joy is to love God and to serve others.

Service can take many forms, but service with a caring heart always leads to significant living. Live to serve, not to be served.

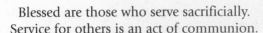

Blessed are those who serve sacrificially.
Service for others is an act of communion.

The wicked trample on the rights of others.
The wise respect the rights of others.

The arrogant ignore the needs of others.
The wise serve the needs of others.

Service for self results in improvement.
Service for others ennobles the one who serves.

The corrupt care little for justice or fairness.
The wise promote justice and pursue fairness.

The selfish live for themselves alone.
The wise live to serve others.

The fool regards service for others
as the means to an end.
The wise regard service for others
as the end in itself.

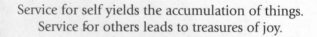

Service for self yields the accumulation of things.
Service for others leads to treasures of joy.

The selfish regard serving others as a "got to" duty.
The wise serve others as a "get to" privilege.

The simple serve others as a burden to bear.
The wise serve others to lift their burdens.

The selfish want to be served.
The wise want to serve.

The corrupt climb lofty heights
on the back of others.
The wise reach lofty heights
by helping others.

The quality of our lives depends upon
the company we keep,
the books we read,
the thoughts we have
and the service we render for others.

Service for Others

"Therefore go and make disciples of all nations,
baptizing them in the name of the Father and of the
Son and of the Holy Spirit, and teaching them
to obey everything I have commanded you."
Matthew 28:19

"So you also, when you have done everything you were
told to do, should say, 'We are unworthy servants;
we have only done our duty.'"
Luke 17:10

"It was he who gave some to be apostles,
some to be prophets, some to be evangelists,
and some to be pastors and teachers,
to prepare God's people for works of service, . . ."
Ephesians 4:11-12

"Serve wholeheartedly,
as if you were serving the Lord. . . ."
Ephesians 6:7

Simplicity and Solitude

We equate success with having a big house, new cars, expensive jewelry, new clothes, a fancy computer and any number of other similar things. But success does not mean more stuff. More stuff is simply more stuff, and having more stuff does not bring us more peace, joy or grace.

"The Lord is my shepherd, I shall not be in want. He makes me lie down in green pastures, he leads me beside quiet waters, he restores my soul."

Psalm 23:1-3

When we learn to simplify our lives, when we get down to the basics, when we are able to shed ourselves of the notion that more stuff is always desirable, we begin to see the possibility of achieving peace. Solitude is a goal, because in the state of solitude, we achieve satisfaction and peace, and in the quiet of solitude, we can hear the whisper of God Himself. We should strive to live our lives with more simplicity, not with more stuff, with more solitude, not with more commotion, with more quiet waters, not with more rapid action; with more grace and joy, not with more honors and rewards.

Simplify your life through regular periods of quiet reflection. Enjoy the joy that flows from making the complex simple.

Simplicity frees the soul
and brings peace to the mind.

Simplicity is achieved by
pursuing purity, holiness and truth.

Simplicity, serenity and solitude
are the keys to spirituality and holiness.

Serenity comes to the man
who abandons himself to find his soul.

The confused speak in riddles.
The wise speak with clarify and simplify.

Water is purified by filtering out impurities.
Man is purified by filtering out self.

The fool knows no purity of heart.
The wise strive for purity through surrender of self.

Seek simplicity, but understand that most situations
are much more complex than they appear.

Quiet complexity.
Seek simplicity.

Silence enables one who listens to really hear.
Silence in the midst of discord is a sign of wisdom.

Clarity and comprehension occur
when complicated things are
simplified into their parts.

Genius is found in making the complex simple,
the obscure clear,
the difficult easy
and the impossible possible.

Order is the essence of the universe.
Silence is the benediction of the soul.

Learn to be silent and listen with your heart.

To find solitude, you must find the quiet place,
the thin place, within your soul
and empty yourself of self.

Simplicity and Solitude

"'In repentance and rest is your salvation,
in quietness and trust is your strength, . . .'"
Isaiah 30:15

"The fruit of righteousness will be peace;
the effect of righteousness will be quietness
and confidence forever."
Isaiah 32:17

"Do not conform any longer to the
pattern of this world, but be transformed
by the renewing of your mind."
Romans 12:2

"The Spirit searches all things, even the deep things
of God. For who among men knows the thoughts
of a man except the man's spirit within him?
In the same way no one knows the thoughts of God
except the Spirit of God. We have not received the
spirit of the world but the Spirit who is from God,
that we may understand what God has freely given us."
1 Corinthians 2:10-12

Success and Significance

Success and significance are quite different. Success generally means that we have made A's in school, we have passed all licensing exams, we have gotten a great job, we are promoted frequently, we have greater and greater responsibility in our jobs and we are being well compensated. Success means winning the race, claiming the victory, receiving the prize.

> *"Be strong and very courageous. Be careful to obey all the law my servant Moses gave you; do not turn from it to the right or to the left, that you may be successful wherever you go."*
>
> Joshua 1:7

Significance does not always translate into success as the world knows it. Significance means making a difference for others, constructing a foundation upon which others can build the future, leaving a legacy of helping others, healing others, giving hope to others and lifting others up. In helping others, abundance may be lost. In healing others, time and resources may be used up. In giving to others, our inventory of resources can get depleted. In lifting others up, we can wear ourselves out. But significance creates peace, joy and hope, things often missing from mere financial or worldly success.

The naive live for temporary success.
The wise live for eternal significance.

Significance is measured not by what a man has
or what he does but by who the man is.

When the wicked succeed,
the righteous wonder why.
When the righteous succeed,
the world knows why.

The intensity of your desire determines
the likelihood of your success.
But a strong desire without persistent
determination will surely fail.

The desire to succeed is a seed to plant.
Commitment, determination and persistence water it.

Significance begins by substituting
humility for pride,
service for possessions, character
for honors and others for self.

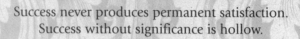

Success never produces permanent satisfaction.
Success without significance is hollow.

Success is measured by
the degree of difficulties overcome to achieve it.

The naive face life as a series of obstacles.
The wise see obstacles as opportunities
for significant living.

The wealthy measure success by counting things.
The wise measure success
by counting people helped.

The lazy give up in the face of tests.
The wise transform trials into triumphs.

The fool works to achieve success.
The wise succeed by finding
significance in those helped.

The proud are too successful to share.
The wise are too significant not to share.

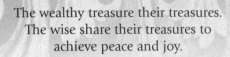

The wealthy treasure their treasures.
The wise share their treasures to
achieve peace and joy.

The fool sees only stumbling blocks.
The wise see stepping-stones.

If you must, you will.
If you do your best, you have not failed.

The first step to reaching your goal is
defining your obective.
Unless you have a goal, you will never reach it.

If you do not have a goal,
any road will take you there.

The lazy do only what is required.
The wise do more than is expected.

Victory is achieved by doing little things greatly.

Success in big things is the result of
many small things done successfully.

Success is generally found only after many failures.

Patience of the wise produces success.
Rash reactions reflect the impotence of the fool.

Financial success has made many men failures.

Achievement does not come to one
who does not believe the goal is possible.

Success happens when focused determination
collides with single-minded effort.

To achieve success, you must first see it,
touch it, sense it and smell it.

The time is never just right.
Start now from where you are with what
you have to become who you want to be.

It is a great mistake to be afraid to make a mistake.
It is a greater mistake to refuse to try.

The best laid plans rest on the answers
to the following questions:
Who? What? When? Where? Why?
How much? How long?

Believing a thing is possible is
a predicate to making it happen.

You can run a marathon if you
continually believe that
you can run past the next tree and
the next parked car and the next stop sign.

Significance is determined not by how much you have,
but by how much you give, how many
you serve and how much you care.

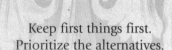

Keep first things first.
Prioritize the alternatives.

Fools do common tasks just to pass inspection.
The wise seek perfection in every task.

The fool accepts mediocrity.
The wise strive for perfection.

Little things done correctly can
lead to great achievement.
Little things done poorly
will always lead to failure.

There is an infinite difference
between good and better,
between better and best.
Choose to seek the best
and reject the rest.

Success and Significance

"Hezekiah trusted in the Lord, the God of Israel.
. . . He held fast to the Lord and did not cease
to follow him; . . . And the Lord was with him;
he was successful in whatever he undertook."
2 Kings 18:5-7

"'Listen to me, Judah and people of Jerusalem!
Have faith in the Lord your God and you
will be upheld; have faith in His prophets
and you will be successful.'"
2 Chronicles 20:20

"Forgetting what is behind and
straining toward what is ahead,
I press on toward the goal to win the prize
for which God has called me
heavenward in Christ Jesus."
Philippians 3:13-14

"I have fought the good fight,
I have finished the race,
I have kept the faith."
2 Timothy 4:7

The very foundation of wisdom is truth. The truth rests upon facts, and facts are often difficult to confirm and often in dispute. Sifting through the rubble and debris of the mess we are in to find the truth is sometimes very difficult. But once the facts are confirmed, the truth will become clear. When you know the truth, the truth will give you wisdom, power and peace.

> *"Surely you desire truth in the inner parts;*
> *you teach me wisdom in the inmost place."*
>
> Psalm 51:6

There are times when we know the truth but do not do it. There are times when we sense the truth but do not pursue it. There are times when we understand the truth but choose to reject it. Honesty involves trusting in the truth and following the truth, even when it hurts, even when no one is watching. Honesty means speaking the truth, walking in the truth and relying upon the truth for no other reason than because it is right to do so.

Follow the truth, and you will achieve integrity. Focus on truth, and you will be set free. Truth often hurts, but failing to pursue truth leads to destruction and despair.

There is no nobler cause than the pursuit of the Truth.

An honest man never finishes last.
The little lie has many brothers and sisters.

Truth is not what we say or do or think.
Truth is what the truth is.

Truth is what actually happens,
not what people say they remember occurred.

Rumors and gossip fan the fires
of conflict and distrust.
Truth stands tall against the storm.

Image is not everything.
Truth is.

Fame is fleeting.
Honesty is enduring.

One lie spoils a life of truth.

Gossip spreads lies and stirs up conflict.
Truth prevails over gossip.

Gossip separates friends.
Truth builds trust.

An honest man's word is his bond.

Fortunes can be made through lies and deception,
but fortunes are trivial and temporary.

A know-it-all never knows it all.

Deception once discovered destroys
credibility for a lifetime.
Honesty and integrity establish respect forever.

Evil and deception are close companions.
Honesty and integrity are marks of the wise.

Corruption and deceit mark the soul of the wicked.
Honesty never produces wicked results.

Treachery and lies poison the wicked.
The wise are filled with truth and compassion.

Curiosity drives creativity.
Curiosity leads to the truth.

Violence and perversity follow the fool.
Peace and truth are companions of the wise.

The bully manipulates the truth.
The wicked pollute the truth.
The wise live the truth.

The fool follows no moral compass.
The wise are grounded in the truth.

Discernment is a gift given to the wise.
Lack of understanding is a trait of the fool.

The proud search others for their vices.
The wise search others for their virtues.

The wicked search others for their vices.
The wise search others for their gifts.

The fool lies to get the prize.
The wise tell the truth because it is right to do so.

Learn the truth and tell it.
Speak the truth and live it.

Do not sacrifice integrity for companionship.
Do not sacrifice truth for temptation.

The corrupt trade integrity for access.
The wise exchange nothing for integrity.

The proud trade goodness for glory.
The wise reject glory for character.

The arrogant reject honesty for power.
The wise have power because of their honesty.

The truth is often inconvenient.
Pursuing the truth in the face of its
inconvenience is noble and right.

An honest man's word is worth
following, believing and embracing.
An honest man is one of God's noblest creations.

The fool desecrates the value of his name.
The wise value a good name above gold.

The naive ignore their conscience.
The conscience of the wise guides their actions.

The frivolous trade truth for fame.
The wise are known for their integrity.

Truth and Honesty

"'These are the things you are to do:
Speak the truth to each other,
and render true and sound judgment
in your courts . . . and do not love
to swear falsely . . .' declares the Lord."
Zechariah 8:16-17

"'If you hold to my teaching,
you are really my disciples.
Then you will know the truth, and
the truth will set you free.'"
John 8:31-32

"Jesus answered, 'You are right in saying I am a king.
In fact, for this reason I was born,
and for this I came into the world,
to testify to the truth.
Everyone on the side of truth listens to me.'"
John 18:37

"For we cannot do anything against the truth,
but only for the truth."
2 Corinthians 13:8

"If we claim to be without sin,
we deceive ourselves and the truth is not in us."
1 John 1:8

Victory and Winning

Winning begins by choosing to participate, working hard to achieve a goal, striving to attain the prize. In most competitions, there are usually those who are stronger, faster, bigger and bolder than you are. But inherent talent does not always carry the day. While winning is the objective of the game, participating with total effort, striving with steadfast commitment, pushing with complete determination is the real victory.

> *"O Lord, the king rejoices in your strength.*
> *How great is his joy in the victories you give!"*
>
> Psalm 21:1

It is in the process of participating, in the act of competing, in taking the risk without assurance of winning the prize that we discover victory. Doing your best under adverse circumstances, reaching beyond your previous limitations and pushing yourself past your extremes is where the true victory is won. True victory means that you have conquered yourself.

So run the journey of life with your whole heart, with your total commitment, with every fiber of your being. By doing so, your victory is assured.

The timid are afraid to lose.
The wise risk losing by trying to win.

The reckless dare others to fight.
The wise win fights by not fighting at all.

If you believe, you can achieve!
If you do not believe, you will not achieve!

Heros are ordinary people
taking extraordinary actions
in the face of seemingly impossible risks.

Victory is not achieved by natural ability alone.
Victory comes through practice,
commitment and discipline.

If you do not practice, do not expect to play.
If you do not play, do not expect to score.
If you do not participate, you cannot win.

The fool is mastered by life.
The wise master life.

Visualize victory to achieve it.

The fool believes that success is final.
The wise know that neither success
nor failure is ever final.

Failure is not falling down but staying down.
Failure is never trying at all.

The greater the opposition,
the more precious the victory.

The goal of the fool is found in the prize.
The goal of the wise is found in the process.

The loser knows pain from losing.
The victor knows pain from discipline and effort.

Life is not about the victory.
Life is about the journey toward victory.

Victory at the expense of others is hollow.
Victory for the benefit of others is significant.

Every large task is the product of many small steps.
Victory requires doing the small things with excellence.

Winning is not everything.
Doing your best is winning, whatever the final score.

Winning is doing God's will to receive God's pleasure.

Defeating your enemy is not victory.
Victory comes when your enemy becomes a friend.

The angry pick fights to win the battle.
The wise avoid fights to win the peace.

You cannot make a good deal with a bad man.
You cannot make a bad deal with a good man.
A good deal is only good if it is good for all.

If a proposal seems too good to be true,
it almost always is.

Praise when work is done.
Console when failure disappoints.
Heal when harm infects.
Support when injury occurs.
Exalt when victory is won.

Winning starts with beginning.
Winners never quit. Quitters never win.

The naive trade life for success.
The wise embrace life to achieve significance.

The timid are afraid to try.
The wise are afraid not to try.

The greatest victory to achieve
is victory over self.

Victory and Winning

"In your majesty ride forth victoriously
in behalf of truth,
humility and righteousness;
let your right hand display awesome deeds."
Psalm 45:4

"With God we will gain the victory,
and he will trample down our enemies."
Psalm 60:12

"The fruit of the righteous is a tree of life,
and he who wins souls is wise."
Proverbs 11:30

"Forgetting what is behind and straining
toward what is ahead, I press on toward
the goal to win the prize for which God
has called me heavenward in Christ Jesus."
Philippians 3:13-14

"I have fought the good fight. I have finished the race.
I have kept the faith."
2 Timothy 4:7

Knowledge is found in accumulating facts, in analyzing those facts and then coming to conclusions based on those facts. Knowledge is all about naming the state capitals of all the states, knowing the chronology of events in various wars, knowing who won the World Series in 1999, describing the process when various chemicals interact and a host of other facts. Knowledge is very important, because without knowledge, man would be lost.

"Blessed is the man who finds wisdom, the man who gains understanding, for she is more profitable than silver and yields better returns than gold. . . . nothing you desire can compare with her."

Proverbs 3:13-15

Knowing facts and using that knowledge to achieve progress, to help others and to inspire future events is wisdom. Wisdom comes from discerning meaning from experience. Wisdom rests upon a knowledge of the relevant facts. But knowledge without wisdom is simply a collection of facts. Wisdom means choosing the best course of action that produces the most good for the most people based on the known facts.

Wisdom results when knowledge of the facts collides with seasoned experience to achieve the highest moral result. Seek knowledge to acquire wisdom to share with others.

Knowledge can be acquired without experience.
Wisdom cannot.

Wisdom seizes the best of our experiences
to achieve the best results.

The action taken which produces
the best results for the greatest number
of people is the wisest action.

There is no shortcut to wisdom.
Wisdom comes by learning from experience.
Experience must be experienced.

One who stops learning is dying.
Ignorance, bigotry and a closed mind
are the opposites of life.

There is power in knowledge.
There is compassion in understanding.
There is peace in wisdom.
There is joy in God's grace.

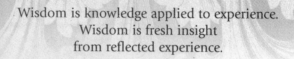

Wisdom is knowledge applied to experience.
Wisdom is fresh insight
from reflected experience.

Wisdom comes from trying,
from suffering the pain of failure,
from persevering in the face
of enormous opposition.

Wisdom comes from knowing God
and experiencing God's pleasure.

Acquiring knowledge for knowledge's sake
profits no one.
Acquiring knowledge to help others profits all.

Zeal without wisdom is like a fire out of control.
Cherish the words of the wise.

It is far better to get wisdom than to
acquire treasures of gold.
It is far better to acquire understanding
than to be honored by kings.

Understanding is a joy to obtain.
Ignorance is a burden to bear.

The son of the fool thinks he
knows everything.
The son of the wise follows
the counsel of the father.

The arrogant learn in order to impress others.
The wise learn in order to serve others.

The road to moral corruption is well traveled.
The road of moral purity is lonely and painful.

Moral integrity is at the very heart of wisdom.

There is no wisdom in the ways of the wicked.
The heart of the corrupt is wicked to the core.

Knowledge is the accumulation of facts.
Wisdom is the application of facts to a moral code.

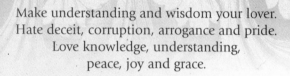

Make understanding and wisdom your lover.
Hate deceit, corruption, arrogance and pride.
Love knowledge, understanding,
peace, joy and grace.

We study to learn facts.
We live to experience wisdom.

Sorrow, envy and strife litter the
path of the proud.
Joy, gratitude and peace fill
the journey of the wise.

When we hear the message,
we forget it quickly.
When we see the message,
we remember it temporarily.
When we experience the message,
we learn it permanently.

Seek knowledge to use it.
Seek wisdom to share it.

Wisdom and Knowledge

"He who walks with the wise grows wise,
but a companion of fools suffers harm."
Proverbs 13:20

"The fear of the Lord teaches a man wisdom,
and humility comes before honor."
Proverbs 15:33

"Oh, the depth of the riches of the wisdom and
knowledge of God! How unsearchable are his
judgments, and his paths beyond tracing out!"
Romans 11:33

"My purpose is that they may be encouraged
in heart and united in love, so that they may
have the full riches of complete understanding,
in order that they may know the mystery of God,
namely, Christ, in whom are hidden all
the treasures of wisdom and knowledge."
Colossians 2:2-3

"If any of you lacks wisdom, he should ask God,
who gives generously to all without finding fault,
and it will be given to him."
James 1:5

Work is a necessary component of every project, every achievement, every endeavor of man. Without work, every idea would simply fall idle, lifeless, without meaning or purpose. Working toward a goal is not only important, but it is absolutely essential if anything is to be accomplished.

"He who works his land will have abundant food, but he who chases fantasies lacks judgment."

Proverbs 12:11

It takes effort to envision the plan. It takes effort to begin the process. It takes effort to overcome obstacles. It takes effort to avoid the pitfalls. It takes effort to achieve goals. Work and effort toward a goal will always prevail over the lazy, the passive and the stagnant. Work and effort will overcome most obstacles and most challenges. Spend the time and exert the effort, and the results achieved will be impressive. Minimize the time and reduce the effort, and the results will reflect it.

Focus your work and your effort to achieve the best possible result, not simply to finish the job. All work should be performed as if God were your client.

Work as hard as you can,
to make as much as you can,
so you can help as many as you can,
so you can give away as much as you can.

If not you, then who?
If not now, then when?

The harder you work,
the luckier you become.

We are made to solve problems,
overcome challenges,
conquer obstacles and
achieve goals.

When your work is a pleasure,
your life will be full of joy.

Achievement requires action, not procrastination.
Without a first step, no journey can begin.

It is much easier to write it long
than to write it short or to write it right.

Every road leads somewhere.
Every trip begins with a first step.

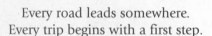

Planning allows the unfolding
events to appear spontaneous.

"Have to" makes the task hard.
"Want to" makes the work fun.

Will power is helpful.
Want power is essential.

Every person has more ability
than he can possibly develop.
Ability not developed is potential left unrealized.

Stagnation results in decay.
Motion prevents stagnation.
Movement without purpose is wasted.
Action toward a goal is progress.

There is joy in creating, building, striving,
doing, working, helping, giving, serving and loving.
There are only excuses in doing nothing.

Purpose pursued with passion produces progress.

Inspiration without perspiration is folly.
Genius involves only a little inspiration
but a lot of perspiration.

To endure in the face of insurmountable difficulties,
to persevere when confronted by impossible odds,
to hold on when hope itself seems hopeless,
that is greatness.

Do more than is expected,
better than is expected,
longer than is expected.

Don't give up. Put up.
Don't give in. Give out.

Embrace the dos.
Avoid the don'ts.

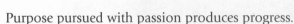

Passion trumps passivity.
Persistence trumps passion.
Perspiration trumps inspiration.
Determination trumps doubt.
Commitment trumps complacency.
Peace trumps passivity.

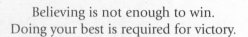

Believing is not enough to win.
Doing your best is required for victory.

Without inspiration, there is no hope.
Without perspiration, there can be no achievement.

Luck is the product of hard work and focused effort.
Luck comes to the diligent, not the lazy.

A lazy man reaps what he sows.
A diligent man never goes hungry.

Worry produces no food.
Work results in a feast for many.

Study today like tomorrow is a final exam.
A moment wasted cannot be relived.

Persistence will prevail over talent,
education over ignorance,
hard work over genius.

Practice always improves performance.
Trying always results in progress.

To have begun by trying,
to have exerted the effort,
to have suffered through the pain of failure,
to have been knocked down, and
to have done your best,
you have surely achieved victory.

Work and Effort

"All hard work brings a profit,
but mere talk leads only to poverty."
Proverbs 14:23

"Moreover, when God gives any man wealth and
possessions, and enables him to enjoy them,
to accept his lot and be happy in his work—
this is a gift of God."
Ecclesiastes 5:19

"Do not work for food that spoils, but for food
that endures to eternal life, . . ."
John 6:27

"Whatever you do,
work at it with your all your heart, . . ."
Colossians 3:23

"'If a man will not work,
he shall not eat.'"
2 Thessalonians 3:10

This collection of ideas, ancient and modern, contain time-tested truths upon which you can stake your life with assurance that truth, wisdom and grace will be your legacy. This collection of ideas is not exclusive nor is it complete. You will find your own truths and your own wisdom by experiencing the application of these and other truths in your life. Search for the truth, and you will receive your reward. Act with wisdom, and you will be blessed and be a blessing to others.

> *"Create in me a pure heart, O God, and renew a steadfast spirit within me."*
>
> Psalm 51:10

Strive to be a role model for those whose lives you touch. Whether young or old, someone is watching you, following you, learning from you. Seek the Truth, and you will find it. Apply the Truth to the obstacles you face, and you will become wise. Do it all to the glory of God, and your life will be filled with joy, peace and abundance of grace.

A point of light bursts through the darkness.
The darkness cannot smother the light.

Beauty is in the heart of compassion,
not in the appearance of the body.

A man is only as sharp as his tact.

Forget mistakes,
but remember the lessons learned from them.

Expect the best.
Reject the rest.

Maximize your attributes.
Minimize your imperfections.

The ignorant fail to read.
The wise read to avoid failing.

To give a successful speech, you need to
show up, stand up, speak up and then shut up.

The lucky attribute their misfortunes to fate.
The wise attribute their good fortune to grace.

Justice delayed is still justice.
Justice never pursued is justice denied.

A father's place is with his son.
A fool squanders the youth of his children.

A father can give his children
protection, provision, education and love.
The rest are incidental details.

A father's affirmation is more powerful
than treasures of gold.
Without a father's affirmation,
the son is adrift on an open ocean of life
without a compass or a rudder.

The naive believe all they read and all they hear.
Confirmation is required by the wise.

A man is known for what he does, not what he thinks.

The arrogant crave power and fame.
The wise seek peace and joy.

The differences between us are very small,
but what a difference those small differences make.

Home is the classroom for greatness.
Parents are the most important teachers.
Children learn best by following an example.

Change is possible only by changing what you hear,
what you see, what you say and what you do.

To have a better world, a better country,
a better state, a better county, a better city,
a better neighborhood, a better church,
and a better family, we must start with
becoming better men and women.

The wise provide light in times of darkness,
guidance in times of doubt and
comfort in times of crisis.

The competitor conquers with
force, skill and determination.
The wise conquer with kindness, character and grace.

Integrity is more important than intelligence.
Service is more important than success.
Gratitude is more important than greatness.
Respect for others is more important
than ruling over others.
Humility is more important than honors.
Peace is more important than pleasure.

A man without vision is a fool without purpose.
Without vision, passion is pointless.
Without passion, vision is mere fantasy.

The wise look past culture and demographics,
title and class, possessions and wealth.
The wise look to the heart and soul.

Hardship produces necessity.
Necessity leads to vision.
Vision gives birth to creativity.
Creativity sparks achievement.
Achievement brings success.
Success finds meaning only in significance.

In everyone you meet, in friends and enemies alike,
try to see their attributes, abilities and worth,
for they like you are unique creations of God.

Each person consists of both pride and spirit.
Look past self to find the soul of a person.

Meditation involves going to the quiet place,
the thin place, the silent space, the place of peace.
In spirit we find the essence of God.

Remember to look for God in everyone,
in everything, everywhere.
Remember that the Spirit of God is found
in the expression of gratitude.

Beyond every storm a rainbow exists.
Following every trial a new beginning arises.
Crisis creates opportunity.
Disaster holds the seeds for future victory.

See yourself as a spiritual being, an eternal creature,
not as a person of physical form only.
Cultivate the spiritual, and your efforts
will lead to joy, peace and grace.

To move forward,
you must move out of your comfort zone.
To move toward significance,
you must move into your creative zone.

The saddest words in all the world are
"what if," "if only," "but if," and "it might have been."

Take time to enjoy the texture of life:
Embrace the tastes, the smells, the sights,
the sounds and the uncertainties of each new day.

Life without the passionate intensity of knowing God
is a life without meaning, purpose or significance.

The passionate pursuit of God's presence
accompanied by service of compassion
to man's needs is God's will for us.

The business of life is not business at all,
but living life to the fullest produces joy.

The greatest victory in life is a life well lived.

A significant life requires:
Health enough to enjoy our work.
Wealth enough to share it with others.
Humility enough to embrace wisdom for others.
Patience enough to learn from the past.
Joy enough to cheer up others.
Service enough to improve the lives of those in need.
Faith enough to embrace the holiness of God.
Hope enough to yearn to see the face of God.
Love enough to touch the heart of God.

Other Truths

"Sanctify them by the truth; your word is truth.
As you sent me into the world,
I have sent them into the world."
John 17:17-18

"Be very careful, then, how you live—
not as unwise but as wise,
making the most of every opportunity,
because the days are evil.
Therefore do not be foolish,
but understand what the Lord's will is."
Ephesians 5:15-17

"Do your best to present yourself to God as one
approved, a workman who does not need to be ashamed
and who correctly handles the words of truth."
2 Timothy 2:15

"But you, keep your head in all situations,
endure hardship, do the work of an evangelist,
discharge all the duties of your ministry."
2 Timothy 4:5

The following is the text of a sermon that I delivered at the Harvard Avenue Methodist Church in Tulsa, Oklahoma on July 13, 2008. In preparing this sermon, I discovered five Biblical principles which answer, at least in part, the question: What is Truth?

John 18:28-38 **Then the Jews led Jesus from Caiaphas to the palace of the Roman governor. By now it was early morning, and to avoid ceremonial uncleanness the Jews did not enter the palace; they wanted to be able to eat the Passover. So Pilate came out to them and asked, "What charges are you bringing against this man?" "If he were not a criminal," they replied, "we would not have handed him over to you." Pilate said, "Take him yourselves and judge him by your own law." "But we have no right to execute anyone," the Jews objected. This happened so that the words Jesus had spoken indicating the kind of death he was going to die would be fulfilled. Pilate then went back inside the palace, summoned Jesus and asked him, "Are you the king of the Jews?" "Is that your idea," Jesus asked, "or did others talk to you about me?" "Am I a Jew?" Pilate replied. "It was your people and your chief priests who handed you over to me. What is it you have done?" Jesus said, "My kingdom is not** of this world. If it were, my servants would fight to prevent my arrest by the Jews. But now my kingdom is from another place." "You are a king, then!" said Pilate. Jesus answered: "You are right in saying I am a king. In fact, for this reason I was born, and for this *I came into the world, to testify to the truth. Everyone on the side of the truth listens to me.* "What is truth?" Pilate asked. [Emphasis added.]

Introduction

I recently had a mind-boggling experience. In June, 2007 I attended an awesome seminar entitled "Mediating the Complex Case" at Pepperdine University. There were 28 very distinguished professionals in my class. Most were full time trial lawyers, but there was also a full time Pepperdine Law School Professor who specializes in Mediation and Dispute Resolution, a former US Attorney for Los Angeles, a psychiatrist/lawyer/family counselor, a former insurance executive, several sitting California state trial judges, the head of all government mediations for New Zealand and the head of all government mediations for Hong Kong. One of our instructors was Teresa Wakeen, who interrupted mediating allegations of sexual misconduct by Catholic priests in Alaska to teach our class. She has previously successfully conducted more than 3,000 other mediations.

Teresa opened Saturday morning's class with a 27 second video. See Surprising Studies of Visual Awareness, www.viscog.com. She said we would see three people on stage dressed in white T shirts and black pants and three other people dressed entirely in black. The people in white shirts were bouncing and passing a white basketball. She asked the class to count the passes and bounces between people in white shirts, saying that a bounce pass counts as one.

She showed the video, and then showed it again. Then she asked, "How many did you get? The answers ranged from 19 to 34. I asked, "Why was there such a disparity in the answers?" I discovered that some of my classmates heard the instruction to be: "Count the passes and the bounces." Others heard the instruction to be: "Count only the changes of possession." Three dribbles and a pass for me was four, but for others three dribbles and a pass was only one. I was convinced that some passes would be from the people wearing white shirts to people in black, just to trick us.

Then Teresa showed the video a third time, this time with new instructions: "Just see what you can see." I was astounded, shocked more accurately. In between the six people on stage walked a woman dressed in a black gorilla suit (without the head) who walked to the middle of the stage, turned and faced the camera, waived and walked out. Not one person in my class saw the gorilla the first two times we saw the video. All of us saw the gorilla the third time.

Teresa explained that people, especially trial lawyers, are often so focused on winning and on answering the question that their minds filter out the obvious, that is, their minds filter out what is black and focus only on what is white in the video. They simply do not see the black gorilla. I persisted, "But what is the right answer?" Teresa looked at me and smiled, "It does not matter." The point, of course, was that mediators should help adverse parties see the "gorilla in the room" as a way of helping them resolve their disputes. Wow!

So what is truth? Was the correct answer 19 or 34 or somewhere in between? Was there a gorilla in the video all three times or just the third time? Is truth what we perceive or is truth sometimes something completely different than what we experience?

Sermon

Since the beginning of time, man has searched for truth. Man has sought truth through nature, through the scientific method, through his analytical mind or through his imagination. Some people explain the mysterious by attributing the unexplained to God. I too want to know the truth.

A Treasury of Truth and Wisdom is a collection of aphorisms, nuggets of truth, short concise statements of principles that contain what I believe are gains of truth. *Treasury* is based upon the premise that what is true should be factual, objective and provable; should be clear, convincing and compelling; and should be fundamental, universal and constant. Truth is not an idea somewhere between two extremes. There is not a plaintiff's truth and a different defendant's truth, and there is not a Republican truth and a different Democratic truth. Truth is truth! But truth is not always what we perceive or what we want.

I heard a story about a journalist writing an article on how different professionals solve problems. The journalist asked a simple question, first to an engineer: "What is four plus three?" The engineer quickly responded, "It's seven you idiot!" The journalist noted that the engineer was precise, specific and unwavering. Then the journalist asked the doctor the same question. The doctor thought for a moment and responded: "I have a pretty good idea, but I need for you to come to my office, let me conduct some tests, I will do some lab work, and then I will tell you my answer." The journalist noted that the doctor was careful, competent and thorough. Then the journalist asked the lawyer: "What is four plus three?" The lawyer responded just as quickly as the engineer: "What do you want it to be?" Truth is truth, no matter who says it, no matter how we spin it and no matter how often we deny it. Four plus three is always seven, the world is not flat, the sun does not revolve around the earth, and man is not God.

Truth can also be mysterious and illusive and may depend upon faith. Man has a brain, but we cannot see it. The wind blows, but we cannot catch it. Gravity exists, and we fall if we ignore it. Love is real, but we cannot measure it, touch it or control it.

Zig Zigler, America's top salesman and a popular motivational speaker says: "Three things I know: There is a God! I ain't Him! You ain't Him either!"

In my search for truth, I turned to the Bible, because according to 2 Timothy 3:16: **"All scripture is God-breathed and is useful for teaching, rebuking, correcting and training in righteousness, so that the man of God may be thoroughly equipped for every good work."**

I discovered five Biblical truths, principles upon which you can trust, you can rely and you can build your life. The first four principles were revealed to me by a friend, Philip Feist, a Bible scholar, former pastor and outstanding Tulsa estate planning lawyer. The fifth may surprise you. It did me.

The first Biblical truth is this: **GOD IS!**

Genesis 1:1 says: **"In the beginning, God...."** Before the stars and the galaxies were; before the heavens and earth existed; before the light was separated from the darkness; before water divided the land; before vegetation, plants and trees existed; before the fish of the sea, the birds of the air, the animals in the field; before man and before woman. God is!

In Exodus 3, Moses was tending sheep when he came to Horeb, the mountain of God, and there Moses saw a burning bush, but the bush was not consumed by the fire. Moses knew immediately that he was standing on holy ground, so he fell on his face. God identified himself as **"I am God of your father, the God of Abraham, the God of Isaac and the God of Jacob."** But Moses was afraid. God then gave Moses a mission to deliver his people the Law and to lead them out of Egypt to the land of milk and honey. But Moses hesitated. Moses needed further assurance, so he asked God to identify Himself. And God said to Moses: **"I AM who I am. This is what you are to tell the Israelites. I AM has sent me to you....This is my name forever, the name by which I am to be remembered from generation to generation."** Exodus 3:14-15.

The Gospel of John confirms this first truth: "In the **beginning was the Word, and the Word was with God and the Word was God. He was with God in the beginning. Through him all things are made; without him nothing was made that has been made.**" John1:1-2

GOD IS THE GREAT "I AM". GOD IS THE "ETERNAL NOW." GOD SIMPLY IS.

The second biblical truth is this: **GOD IS HOLY!**

Man has sensed from the beginning that there is one or more gods, forces beyond himself that exist and that influence his life. The earliest tribes found God in the unexplainable forces of nature. They worshipped the sun, the moon, the stars, the land, water, fire and air. The ancient Greeks created a god for everything: War, peace, beauty, wine, etc.

Modern man attributes to God various characteristics: He is creator. He is omniscient. He is omnipotent. God is everywhere and is in all things. He is a Mighty Judge. He is our Redeemer. He is Abba. He is the compassionate Prodigal Father, ever forgiving, ever seeking, ever loving us back to Him. One thing is sure: God deserves to be worshipped, because **GOD IS HOLY!**

Listen to the following examples from Scripture that confirm this fundamental truth:

Leviticus 11:45: **"I am the Lord who brought you up out of Egypt to be your God; therefore be holy, because I am holy."** Isaiah 44:6: **"I am the first and I am the last; apart from me there is no God."** Psalm 99:9: **"Exalt the Lord our God and worship at his holy mountain, for the Lord our God is holy."** Revelation 4.8: **"Holy, holy, holy is the Lord God Almighty, who was, and is and is to come."** There can be no doubt: **GOD IS HOLY!**

The third Biblical truth is this: **GOD COMES.**

God comes to all mankind collectively. Listen to Genesis 1:27-28: **"So God created man in his own image, in the image of God he created him; male and female he created them. God blessed them and said to them: 'Be fruitful and increase in number; fill the earth and subdue it. Rule over the fish of the sea and the birds of the air and every living creature that moves on the ground.'"**

God also comes to individuals. Here are some Biblical examples: In Genesis 12, God came to Abraham at the age of seventy-five, so that Abraham might become the father of our faith. In Exodus 3, God came to Moses in a burning bush to give Moses the Law and to commission Moses to lead the displaced Jewish people out of Egypt to the Promised Land. In 1 Samuel 18, God came to David, the least among even his seven brothers, a lowly shepherd boy from the poorest town in all of Judea, to unite the twelve Jewish tribes as their king and to write most of the Psalms. In Luke 1:39-55, God came to Mary, a poor teenage peasant girl, to lift her above all women and to choose her to become the mother of Jesus. In Matthew 4, God came to the twelve disciples, ordinary men, who were available and upon whom God built his Church. In Acts 9:1-7, God came to Paul on the road to Damascus to blind him and transform him from being a passionate persecutor to becoming a great disciple and the author of one-third of the New Testament.

Paul writing to the Romans reached the same conclusion: **"For there is no difference between Jew and Gentile—the same Lord is Lord of all and richly blesses all who call him, for everyone who calls on the name of the Lord will be saved."** Romans 10:12-13

I have a friend who publishes the Community Spirit newspaper in Tulsa. Tom McCloud's business card has a two of clubs on the back. The two of clubs is the lowest card in the deck. Why? So that he can tell how God uses ordinary people, often people who are seen as the lowest in the social and religious order. God does not necessarily use the most qualified, but God always qualifies the most available, even if they represent the two of clubs.

God also comes to you and me. God comes to us through the natural world. His beauty, majesty and power are all around us. God comes to us through the life of Jesus, His Son and our Savior. God comes to us through His Bible. God comes to us through our prayers. God comes to us through others who know Him. God comes to us when we surrender to him. God comes to us through that "still small voice" within us—God's Holy Spirit.

When Jesus was nearing the end of His ministry on earth, his disciples were greatly distressed. To calm their fears, Jesus said to them in John 14:15, 18: **"If you love me, you will obey what I command. And I will ask the Father, and he will give you another Counselor to be with you forever—the Spirit of Truth...I will not leave you as orphans; I will come to you."**

Through the mysterious vision received by John and recorded in Revelation, God revealed His message to all who believe. In Revelation 22:12, Jesus said to John: **"Behold, I am coming soon! My reward is with me, and I will give to everyone according to what he has done. I am the Alpha and Omega, the First and the Last, the Beginning and the End."**

God not only comes to us, but God reaches out to us and invites us to come home to where He is. Revelation 22:16-17, Jesus said: **"I, Jesus have sent my angel to give you this testimony for the churches. I am the Root and the Offspring of David, and the bright Morning Star. The Spirit and the bride say, "Come!" ...let him take the free gift of the water of life."** The third truth is confirmed throughout the Bible. **GOD COMES!**

The fourth Biblical truth is this: **GOD CALLS!**

God did not simply set the world in motion and leave it. God lives. God is directly involved with His world and is directly involved with each of us. God is personal. God calls each of us to fulfill our unique purpose, our call.

Listen to our mission call. **"And we know that in all things God works for the good of those who love him, who have been called according to his purpose. For those God foreknew, he also predestined to be conformed to the likeness of his Son, that he might be the firstborn among many brothers. And those he predestined, he also called; those he called, he also justified; he also glorified."** Romans 8:28-30

We are called to love God and to serve others. "What is the greatest commandment in the law," asked the

Jewish lawyers. Jesus replied: "**Love the Lord your God with all your heart and with all your soul and with all your mind. This is the first and greatest commandment. And the second is like it: 'Love your neighbor as yourself.' All the Law and the Prophets hang on these two commandments.**" Matthew 22:37-39

More personally, Jesus gave us His Great Commandment to go into the whole world, to make disciples of all peoples, to baptize them and to teach them the Word and the ways of Christ. Matthew 28:19. We are to trust Him and obey Him. There simply is no other way.

Finally, the fifth Biblical truth I learned is this: **GOD IS TRUTH!**

God's Word is truth. After the Last Supper, Jesus prayed three prayers: One for Himself, one for the disciples and one for all believers. In His prayer for the disciples, Jesus prayed: "**My prayer is not that you take them [the disciples] out of this world but that you protect them from the evil one. They are not of this world, even as I am not of it. Sanctify them by the truth: your Word is truth.**" John 17:15-17

God's Holy Spirit is truth. In John 16:7,12, Jesus explained to his disciples that it is good for them that Jesus should return to God. Jesus said this. "**But I tell** you truth: It is for your good that I am going away. Unless I go away, the Counselor will not come to you....But when he, the Spirit of truth, comes, he will guide you into all truth." God's Spirit is truth!

Finally and most importantly, Jesus himself is truth. At the last supper, Jesus prayed for his disciples: **"Do not let your hearts be troubled. Trust in God; trust also in me. In my Father's house are many rooms....I am going there to prepare a place for you."** When Thomas asked the way, Jesus said: **"I am the way, the truth and the life. No one comes to the Father except through me."** John 14:1-6 Jesus, God's Son, is Truth!

Therefore, God's Word is truth. God's Spirit is truth. God through His Son is truth.

So why is Truth so important for you and me today? Jesus answered this question also. In speaking about those who believe in Him, Jesus said: **"If you hold to my teaching, you are really my disciples. Then you will know the truth and the truth will set you free."** John 8:31-32

GOD IS! GOD IS HOLY! GOD COMES! GOD CALLS! GOD IS TRUTH!

Invitation

Therefore, if you want to be free, you must know the Truth. Since Jesus is Truth, you must know Jesus. If we surrender who we are in order to become like Him, if we trust Him and obey His Word, we will find the Truth, and Jesus will set us free indeed!

If you do not know Jesus in a personal way, I urge you not to leave here today without becoming acquainted with Him. You can know Him if you simply ask Him to come into your heart. Come and ask.

Prayer of Surrender

Lets us pray. Father, some of us are slaves to addictions that consume and control us. Some of us are suffering from physical, emotional or spiritual pain. Others of us are slaves to our jobs, slaves to our money, slaves to things. All of us are slaves to our pride. All of us are broken, bruised, baffled, bewildered, busted and battered by this world. Nothing we do sets us free.

We have learned today that Jesus is Truth, and Truth sets us free. Today, we accept Jesus, your Son, as our Savior and as our Truth. We confess that we need Him more today than ever before. We surrender who we are to become more like who He is. Come, heal us, forgive us and set us free. In the name of Jesus, we pray. Amen.

Now that you know some of the truth, what are you going to choose to do? Are you going to follow a life of pursuing things or will you seek spiritual and sacred solitude? Will you avoid adversity by choosing to listen and accept the advice of the wise? Will you give yourself in service to others, or will you continue to choose to pursue more money and more stuff? Will you dwell on your past achievements and fail to take the risks that could lead to a life of the rewards of peace and solitude, gratitude and grace? The choice is yours. What will you choose?

Throughout history, man has tried to discern the will of God in order to live according to God's ways. We say that if we only knew what God wanted us to do, we would do it. But the fact is, most of the time we do know what God's will is for us. The great mystery is why we do not do it.

A good summary of a life of truth, wisdom, peace and joy is found in the following simple but powerful comments of Moses, David, Solomon and Jesus. If you accept their comments, you will find the greatest treasury of truth and wisdom ever discovered. To God be the glory!

Long ago, Moses summarized the law of truth and wisdom this way:

"These are the commands, decrees and laws the Lord your God directed me to teach you to observe . . . Hear, O Israel: The Lord our God, the Lord is one. Love the Lord your God with all your heart and with all your soul and with all you strength." (Deuteronomy 6:1,4-5)

David, the greatest king of Israel and author of most of the Psalms, was a man who sought the heart of God. When David was only a boy, Goliath, the Philistine giant, confronted the army of Israel. David announced to King Saul with assurance that God would protect David against Goliath:

"The Lord who delivered me from the paw of the lion and the paw of the bear will deliver me from the hand of this Philistine." (1 Samuel 17:37)

Solomon, son of David, often regarded as the world's wisest and richest man, wrote the Book of Proverbs early in his life to teach men how to act and how to live. But Solomon strayed from God's way. In his old age, Solomon began the Book of Ecclesiastes with this admonition: **"Everything is meaningless"** (Ecclesiastes 1:2), especially possessions, pleasures and riches, even knowledge and wisdom. He concluded Ecclesiastes with these words: **"Fear God and keep his commandments, for this is the whole duty of man."** (Ecclesiastes 12:13)

Jesus, Son of God and son of Man, came into this world not just to teach us God's ways, but He came to be our model of God's way. Jesus said:

> "'Love the Lord your God with all your heart and with all your soul and with all your mind.' This is the first and greatest commandment. And the second is like it: 'Love your neighbor as yourself.' All the Law and the Prophets hang on these two commandments." (Matthew 22:37-40)

Jesus also said, "If you hold to my teaching, you are really my disciples. Then you will know the truth, and the truth will set you free." (John 8:31-32) Note that knowing the truth is not enough. We must know the truth *and* live it. It is in living the truth that we find significance, joy and peace beyond our wildest expectations.

The teachings of Moses, the lessons of David and Solomon and the example of Jesus summarize unchanging principles of truth and wisdom. Follow these truths, and you will live a life beyond success to significance.

One Final Thought

There is no trouble too great,
no humiliation too deep,
no suffering too severe,
no labor too hard,
no expense too large,
no love too strong,
but that it is worth it,
if it is spent to win a soul.

Betty Broding Luceigh
May 1961

Index of Biblical Passages Cited

Frederick K. Slicker is a business lawyer in Tulsa, Oklahoma. He holds a Bachelor of Arts degree in Mathematics from the University of Kansas (1965), a Juris Doctor degree with highest distinction from the University of Kansas Law School (1968), and a Masters of Law degree from Harvard University Law School (1973).

Fred is the author of three other books: A *Practical Guide to Church Bond Financing*, a guide for churches in conducting church bond programs in compliance with federal and state securities laws; *Angels All Around*, an autobiography of his life in the practice of law; and *Seeking God's Heart: A Devotional Journey Through the Psalms*, a daily devotional based upon the Psalms.

Fred is a co-founder of First Men, the men's ministry at First United Methodist Church in Tulsa, and an active leader in various local men's ministry programs, including Promise Keepers and the National Center for Fathering. He is a frequent continuing legal education speaker. Fred is also a mediator of complex legal disputes, especially disputes involving commercial issues.

Fred and his wife, Claudia, have two children, Laura Mayes, a lawyer and mother of Eli Lucas Mayes, residing with her husband, Luke, in Powder Springs, Georgia, and Kipp, a medical student residing with his wife, Chris, in Tulsa.